Kingdom Leadership

Lessons Learned to Impact Our World

Kingdom Leadership: Lessons Learned To Impact Our World.

Printed in the United States of America

Published by:
Mall Publishing Co.
www.MallPublishing.biz
877.203.2453

Cover and text design by Susan P. Kramer

Edited by Martha Rankin, Associate Writer and RIMI partner

ISBN: 978-1934165-69-0 1-934165-69-7

For licensing/copyright information, additional copies, or for use in specialized settings contact:

Reaching Indians Ministries International (RIMI)

1949 Old Elm Road
Lindenhurst IL 60046
USA

Phone: 847.265.0630
Fax: 847.265.0642
Email: ministry@rimi.org
Website: www.RIMI.org/

Kingdom Leadership

Lessons Learned to Impact Our World

Saji Lukos

WHAT OTHER LEADERS ARE SAYING

Of the many leadership books that fall neatly into the categories of biblical and/or corporate, Dr. Saji Lukos provides a much-needed balanced perspective in his latest book, ***Kingdom Leadership***. Weaving scriptural principles and life experiences around a kingdom perspective gives readers a glimpse of authenticity and reproducibility often found missing in the glut of popular leadership books on the market today. His chapter on spousal support of vision is especially noteworthy!

Dr. John Strubhar
Interim Pastor's Ministry First Baptist Church
Merced, CA

In ***Kingdom Leadership*** Saji Lukos shares from his life's preaching and teaching a dozen pithy principles of Christian leadership that are foundational, functional and fruitful.

Dr. T.V. Thomas
Chairman, Global Diaspora Network (GDN)

Dr. Saji Lukos' new book, ***Kingdom Leadership*** is truly born out of life and leadership lessons he learned and applied in his ministry from its inception. As Saji responded to God's calling and obeyed the Holy Spirit, he learned the ***Kingdom Leadership*** principles outlined in this book that has impacted countless lives. It is a "must read" for anyone impassioned to be a Kingdom leader.

Ernest Mall, President
Mall Publishing Co.

Dr. Saji Lukos is a dynamic teacher, and I have had the privilege of attending his sessions; but he is also a keen learner. In Kingdom Leadership: *Lessons Learned to Impact Our World*, Dr. Lukos shares with us the richness of leadership that can only come from a lifetime of learning. I wholeheartedly endorse this book by Dr. Saji Lukos, whose life and leadership has positively impacted thousands around the world

Rev. Vijayesh Lal / Executive Director
Evangelical Fellowship Of India

Lukos has done it again. To read this powerful book with an open mind and obedient heart will transform the reader, the church and the world! This book is important reading for searching and hungry leaders.

Robert J. Schill, AIA, CSI, NCARB, Architect
Volunteer Missionary Architect Globally

Dr. Saji Lukos has clearly articulated ***Kingdom Leadership*** insights from his personal journey together with God and His people. Read it and be blessed.

Rev. Dr. Richard Howell
General Secretary Asia Evangelical Alliance;
Executive Secretary: EFI Council of Churches.

I have had the privilege of being a good friend of and collaborator with Saji since 2000. What you will discover in his new book are passionate *life lessons* turned into *principles* that Saji has consistently delivered as *teachings* to others over time. When I reflect on my friend I consistently observe two profound characteristics of this remarkable leader of men and women: first, Saji has "single-minded" focus. He lives every waking hour of every day advancing the incremental details of the Big Picture of RIMI-MI. He thinks big, but works diligently on the small details; and secondly, anyone who has ever spent even a few hours with Saji will know that he is always "asking" for something from you to help advance the Big Picture. The chapter "Ask Courageously" is well worth the read.

Thomas P. Dooley, Ph.D.
Biomedical Entrepreneur and Founder of Path Clearer
www.PathClearer.com

Saji Lukos is a leader's leader. When I first met him as a pastor I sensed a deeply godly man who had the uncanny ability to attract young gifted leaders. What draws people to Saji is his character. Character isn't gained through mere intellectual exercises; it's forged by biblical truth that penetrates into the depths of the human heart. Saji is first and foremost a man that spends time with God, and thus his character has been shaped and molded by the hours on his knees and by hours of meditating on God's Word. In ***Kingdom Leadership***, Saji is not just enumerating principles; he is giving the life lessons that radically transformed him into a man that God could entrust with one of the most effective ministries in all of India. This book is textbook on how you, too, can translate your vision and passion into a force for the Kingdom of God. I highly recommend this book! Thank you, Saji. I have learned much from you, brother, both in our travels and by observing your life in Christ.

Tom Doyle Vice-President and Middle East Director
for e3 Partners- Author of *Killing Christians-Living the Faith where it is NOT Safe to Believe*

I have had the privilege of knowing Saji and Mony Lukos for over twenty years now, first providing simple technical support in RIMI's early days, then serving on the RIMI Board of Directors. As I have observed his dealings here in the US, and during my visits to the ministry in India, I have never once had cause to question these things:

Saji's absolute devotion to Jesus;
Saji's radical passion to see people take up their proper place in service of God's Kingdom; and
Saji's genuine love for the people he meets and serves.

I offer these observations not to build up Saji, but to say that the lessons recounted in this book are genuine and are tested out by Saji in his personal dealings time and again.

I offer this warning: Don't spend time with Saji in person or via this book unless you are willing to bare your soul to God and wonder what more He may have in store for you in your Kingdom tasks, wherever you have opportunity to lead.

Dennis Clements
Minister of Music Aldersgate United Methodist Church
Huntsville, AL 35761

When you read this volume it rings a bell of truth in your spirit. If you've met the author Saji Lukos, you know the leadership truths contained in this book is personified in his life. By God's grace, Saji has thus far been empowered to practice what he preaches in these pages. I challenge you to go and do the same."

Michael Allen
Senior Pastor, Uptown Baptist Church
Chicago

Dr. Saji has drawn on his years of experience to offer us a clear view of ***Kingdom Leadership***. His broad experience in leadership and his love of sharing and teaching are skillfully combined in the impactful pages you are about to read.

Dr. Brent Davis
Professor of Management and Pastor

The quintessence of the book *Kingdom Leadership* is the life and witness of Dr. Saji Lukos. Three enlightening principles I acquired from this book: 1. Lovelessness is Self & Selflessness is Love. 2. Living for others is heaven upon earth and living for self is hell upon earth. 3. *"Leadership should mean giving control rather than taking control and creating leaders rather than forging followers"*. - (David Marquet)

The praxis of this book by any reader will certainly give impetus to "Glocal" approach (Glocal = Global+Local) in transforming local and global communities for the glory of God's Kingdom. I praise God and thank Him to be born in this generation to serve God in Dr. Saji Lukos' team who is my leader, mentor and guide.

Premjit Kumar
Director: Mission India Bible College,
Warangal, India

"Dr. Saji Lukos has written a most helpful book – one that leaders in all walks of ministry can benefit from. His own experiences as a ministry visionary and leader add a depth and richness to the principles that are timeless. Highly recommended!"

Dr. Carl A. Moeller
CEO, Biblica

Very few people become the embodiment of the Gospel narrative. Dr. Saji Lukos is among the exception. His tireless work, humility and visionary leadership has taken RIMI to be among the largest of evangelical organizations in the world. In *Kingdom Leadership: Lessons Learned to Impact Our World*, you see this journey of a servant of God sold out for the purposes of God. Thank you for supporting my friend Dr. Saji's vision.

Sujo John,
Inspirational Speaker/ Founder –
You Can Free Us Foundation, Dallas, Texas

Most leadership books offer little to the reader because the author talks about leadership. In *Kingdom Leadership*, Saji Lukos lives out leadership. The difference is dramatic. Join the journey with Saji and you will collect valuable nuggets for your leadership role.

J. Paul Nyquist, Ph.D.
President, Moody Bible Institute

To study leadership you must have a desire to change. To teach it you must have been transformed. A book written by one who has lived a journey of change and transformation then is practically significant and a requisite for our corrupted times. Personally I know of very few whose very life embodies the principles of prayer, vision, courage, credibility and confidence. Using his own story Dr. Saji Lukos connects us with His Story through *Kingdom Leadership*. Nicely done!!!

Krish Dhanam
Managing Partner Skylife Success
Co-author of *Hard Headed and Soft Hearted*
and contributing author to
Top Performance written by Zig Ziglar

DEDICATION

This book is dedicated to Annamma Lukos, my beloved mother, who passed away in August 2015. I was able to learn about Kingdom leadership principles because of her devotion to Christ, sincere prayers, her steadfast faith in the Lord, and her sacrifice to raise her eight children amidst her many health challenges. I owe more to my mother than I can express in words, as well as my gratitude to God for her precious life.

Table of Contents

ACKNOWLEDGEMENTS

Thanks to Martha Rankin, my precious sister and encourager in the Lord, who has assisted me in writing this book. Martha used Hadley Hoover's editorial services for this book, and so, to Hadley, a big thank you as well. Martha and Hadley became better friends during the process of working together, and this is an added blessing both to them and to me.

Thanks to my close friend and partner in the ministry Pastor Jeff Whitt, Senior Pastor of New Hope Evangelical Free Church, who has graciously written the Forward of this book. Also thanks to Pastor Jerry Foote, my good friend, mentor, and former Chairman of the RIMI Board, for his input on ***Kingdom Leadership***.

I am also grateful to my wife Mony and daughter Maryann for their labor with me in fulfilling the vision that God has entrusted to the ministry of RIMI. We are apart during my numerous travels to many nations, especially to India, and we miss each other very much during these times. Their encouragement and constant prayers have inspired me to go many, many extra miles in representing our King-Lord Jesus Christ.

FOREWORD

I have known Saji Lukos since 1990 when we were fellow students in the Masters of Divinity program at Trinity Evangelical Divinity School (TEDS) in Deerfield, Illinois—and in our 20's! Since that time, I have known and observed Saji in a full range of activities and roles: as student, husband, father, son, sibling, preacher, ministry leader, movement leader, bus driver and more! I have had the great privilege of watching as the Lord has revealed and developed these leadership lessons in Saji's life over what is now a quarter of a century.

One of Saji's most valuable roles as the leader of a movement and a large network of churches in India and Southeast Asia is to cast a vision for the gospel and the Great Commission. Few people have lived, loved and worked among such an amazing socio-economic and cultural diversity of God's people as Saji, who travels extensively particularly in Asia and North America. His first book, *Transformed for a Purpose*, motivates those who know Christ to greater faithfulness in seeking to make Christ known among all the peoples of the earth.

I know of no one who more honestly and persuasively calls others with a Holy Spirit–inspired urgency to turn from sin and to Christ, and then to live out and pass on the gospel in the home, business and local church, than does Saji. His first book casts that big, all-important vision.

This book—*Kingdom Leadership: Lessons Learned to Impact Our Word* is a natural follow-up in which my dear friend looks back on the 30-plus years he has walked with God. In it, he identifies and explains 12 core principles which God has taught him about gospel-empowered leadership.

It is clear that these lessons have emerged from Saji's lifelong experiences of loving people and leading churches, businesses and mercy homes in several countries and cultures. It is also clear that they are like sifted gold, condensed from much more that he could say. I*n Kingdom Leadership: Lessons Learned to Impact Our Word*, Saji calls us to live out God's purpose through lives which are in tune with the 12-part symphony of incarnational leadership that he commends in this book.

I am one of hundreds who can attest that Saji lives out what he teaches (including repenting when he doesn't!) However, what makes this book particularly special is that its message flows out of a worshipful gaze on Jesus as the unique and supreme Lord and Savior. Its teaching is built solely on the foundation of the Bible as the very Word of God. This means that as you read this book you will not only be helped as a leader, but also compelled to worship Jesus more intelligently, passionately and wisely.

You will not only be motivated in certain aspects of leadership, but also encouraged to base your life more wholeheartedly on the clear teachings of God's written Word. Saji's leadership lessons are ultimately not his, even though they are often illustrated through his life and the ministry of RIMI/MI (Reaching Indians Ministries International/Mission India). This book is the overflow of Saji's worship of Jesus as unique Savior and Lord and arises out of his deep reflection on and full surrender to the absolute authority of the Bible.

I desperately need what this book commends and so do all of God's people and churches! We need to be reminded of the wide variety of diverse and complementary leadership qualities that Jesus modeled and which His Spirit seeks to develop in His people.

Although Saji unapologetically shares these truths against the backdrop of his life, he longs to see gospel- empowered incarnational leadership spring up in every culture and location. He longs to see thousands of people lead in the manner that flows from Jesus and the Bible, by unknown leaders in little hidden ways and a few well-known leaders in very public ways. May this book play its part in developing and deploying those kinds of leaders!

For the glory of God, the joy of God's people and the good of all the nations!

Jeff Whitt
Senior Pastor, New Hope Evangelical Free Church, Orange City, Iowa

INTRODUCTION

This book was born out of a leadership seminar Dr. Saji Lukos was asked to give at New Hope Evangelical Free Church in Orange City, Iowa, in April 2014. While on his knees asking God to guide him in his teaching on leadership, and how to present to the 50-plus church leaders who were coming to attend a seminar on Godly leadership, Saji was given by God this list of qualities in Kingdom-style leadership.

As he prepared a PowerPoint presentation on this topic, Justin Schuiteman (his helper, in whose family home he was staying) told him that he should write a book on this subject. Here it is.

The word "leadership" brings up images of great people who have invested time and energy into others and who have poured into others hard-earned expertise and guidance.

When the word "Kingdom" is used to describe this style of leadership, the whole meaning or definition changes.

What are those often elusive qualities needed to be a Godly leader with abilities that are pleasing to your most holy and righteous God, and yet speak into the hearts of fellow believers?

What are the rules that can be applied to be who God designed you to be from before the beginning?

For answers to these questions, one can look at lessons learned in Saji's life and his desire to serve others—lessons learned for the fame of the One he serves.

As Dr. Lukos reflected on the grace of God in his life since accepting Jesus Christ as his personal Savior in 1979, he knew these qualities were from the Christ he had come to love and serve. He recognized the way God was preparing him to do ministry.

God began to remind him of the things he had learned over the years from ups and downs in the ministry—the successes and failures—which have shaped his life and leadership style. All he had learned from his life experiences, he could now look at in retrospect and see how God was leading, guiding, and preparing him all along for His plan in His Kingdom.

He has learned lessons from other respected Godly leaders as well. The world is full of leaders of all kinds, but Saji found that in over 30 years of ministry since the 1970s, there are 12 guiding principles that have shaped his leadership.

All of these are interwoven with prayerfully making the glory of Christ known to the nations—especially to the least-reached peoples of his beloved home country of India and throughout Southeast Asia.

Saji's principles—lived and learned from hard, yet God-directed, life experiences—form the chapters of this book:

1. Begin with Christ
2. Establish credibility at home
3. Identify your destiny
4. Pray specifically
5. Dream a God-sized vision
6. Be faithful in the little things
7. Build your team
8. Risk your life for others
9. Ask courageously
10. Have a Kingdom perspective
11. Have absolute confidence in God
12. And spouse shares the vision

~ Martha Rankin,
Associate Writer and Partner of RIMI

CHAPTER 1

Begin with Christ

Believing the right things about Jesus isn't enough. You're not adopted as God's child until you confess and turn away from your wrongdoing and receive the freely offered gift of forgiveness and eternal life that Jesus purchased with his death on the cross. Until you do that, you'll always be on the outside looking in.

– Lee Strobel

My name has been Saji since my physical life began at birth. The life ordained for me by my Creator, however, began when I had a life-changing encounter with Christ and my name was written in the Book of Life.

Simply put, but profoundly accurate: Christ is my life. Before beginning a relationship with Christ, I had no hope or peace. I began to really *live* only after I met Jesus Christ.

Yes, I was "alive" in the physical sense before I gave control of all aspects of my life to Christ. I had been born into a family in Kerala state, India. But my existence was often miserable and my spiritual life was dead.

I knew little joy. My family was in turmoil. They (including me) believed in God, but only as a far off, impersonal entity. To us, God had little to no interest in our personal lives or circumstances. Daily life depended on how much we could work to attain what was necessary, but none of it had anything to do with a relationship, or dependence on, God.

We were not Hindus or Muslims, so we were considered "Christians." However, "being a Christian" meant more what we were *not* rather than what we *were*. The word "Christian" had no personal meaning as to who one was "in Christ." Rather, it carried the meaning of not being a part of one of the other religions in the country of India. Knowing Jesus as a personal Savior involved in every aspect of daily life –this was not part of the Lukos family mentality.

I myself came to know Jesus personally; but instead of being pleased, this angered my father to the point that for safety reasons I soon had to leave home. This story was told in my previous book, ***Transformed for a Purpose***, which relates my journey from a new believer in Christ to the eventual spiritual healing of my whole family, including the salvation of my father who at first beat me because of my beliefs in Christ—beliefs which gave the designation of "Christian" its truest meaning.

Another God-ordained result of my conversion was the birth of two ministries: Mission India (MI) and Reaching Indians Ministries International (RIMI) that I have been privileged to found and watch grow. I attribute my viewpoint of serving God and doing ministry with and through Him to this passage from the Apostle Paul's epistle to the church in Corinth:

> *Therefore, since through God's mercy we have this ministry, we do not lose heart. Rather, we have renounced secret and shameful ways; we do not use deception, nor do we distort the Word of God. On the contrary, by setting forth the truth plainly we commend ourselves to everyone's conscience in the sight of God. And even if our Gospel is veiled, it is veiled to those who are perishing. The god of this age has blinded the*

minds of unbelievers, so that they cannot see the light of the Gospel that displays the glory of Christ, who is the image of God. For what we preach is not ourselves, but Jesus Christ as Lord, and ourselves as your servants for Jesus' sake. For God, who said, "let light shine out of darkness," made His light shine in our hearts to give us the light of the knowledge of God's glory displayed in the face of Jesus Christ.

But we have this treasure in jars of clay to show that this all-surpassing power is from God and not from us. We are hard pressed on every side, but not crushed; perplexed, but not in despair; persecuted, but not abandoned; struck down, but not destroyed. We always carry around in our body the death of Jesus, so that the life of Jesus may also be revealed in our body. For we who are alive are always being given over to death for Jesus' sake, so that His life may also be revealed in our mortal body. So then death is at work in us, but life is at work in you.

[II Corinthians 4:1-12. NIV]

I admit to having discouraging times in my ministry; but my prayer and attitude are ones of thankfulness for these blessings from the hand of my loving and merciful Father: i.e.,

- the ministry I have been ordained to do, called to do, and equipped for
- my wife, Mony, and daughter, Maryann
- the people of India
- my parents, brothers and sisters
- my team members
- all those whom God used to bless me so richly, including

the hundreds of people who have invested in me as I learned the spiritual lessons of leadership.

None of my growth would have been possible unless I had taken the first step to begin with God—giving my heart, desires, ambitions and everything that encompasses life over to Jesus Christ. This gave me the Kingdom perspective I have endeavored to keep since the day capital-L *Life* that keeps eternity's values in view truly began. That day, I began to allow God to form me into the leader He wanted me to be and the leader I continue to strive to be today.

Leadership begins with Christ. Christ equips people to fulfill His global plan for all the peoples of the earth. Christ is the source for leadership style. When a believer begins life in Christ, He becomes, is, and must remain, the leader. When a believer chooses to follow Christ, he is to emulate Him and lead like He does, or more correctly, to allow Him to lead through him. True Kingdom-style leadership is this: to put self under the Lordship of Christ, Who leads as a servant, and not to try to get ahead by leading without Him.

The Kingdom of God is not merely the sovereignty of God over creation, but also and specifically God's ruling of creation through His human representatives. He does not enlist us to be subjects of His Kingdom, but to be co-rulers with Him in the transformation of the creation that is being spoiled by sin.

As I examined my own life prior to beginning to teach others about leadership principles, I could see my life began when Jesus Christ gave my life meaning. Hope was nonexistent before I met Christ.

At the urging of a distant relative, two evangelists—John Ninan and A.V. Thomas—came to the room where I was staying and shared the basic Gospel of Jesus Christ with me. That day, I began a journey that had been ordained by God before the foundations of the world were formed.

Within a few days after repeated visits from A.V. and John, I yielded my life to Christ. That was the day I—Saji Lukos, God's child and His new creation and a Kingdom worker—truly began to live.

Until that time, I had never known or found peace, despite my searching. I didn't even have my own Bible! I knew nothing about what God said through divinely inspired writers; but in my hunger as a new Christian for God's Word, I began to find spiritual food in the Bible and learned what was important in my new life. As Jesus said:

> *And fear not them which kill the body, but are not able to kill the soul: but rather fear him which is able to destroy both soul and body in hell. Are not two sparrows sold for a farthing? And one of them shall not fall on the ground without your Father. But the very hairs of your head are all numbered.*
>
> [Matthew 10:28-30. KJV]

These verses helped me learn how important I was to God. I had never experienced significance before. Further reading and Bible study taught me that I had Someone in Whom I could put my trust—a Divine Someone Who cared about everything concerning me.

> *Come unto me, all ye that labor and are heavy laden, and I will give you rest. Take my yoke upon you, and learn of me; for I am meek and lowly in heart: and ye shall find rest unto your souls. For my yoke is easy, and my burden is light.*
>
> [Matthew 11:28-30. KJV]

I had joy never felt before in the previous 20 years. Ancient holy words spoke to my heart and explained what I was feeling—and the Psalmist's words have remained a constant for me – to wit:

> *Thou hast put gladness in my heart, more than in the time their corn and their wine increased. I will both lay me down in peace, and sleep: for thou, LORD, only makest me dwell in safety.*
>
> [Psalm 4:7-8. KJV]

When I was first asked to give testimony to my new-found faith in Christ. I quoted these very verses. An English translation of the Indian Bible puts it so beautifully: "More than the rice fields and wealth of my family I will be given joy." I understand and feel this; it speaks to my heart. Almighty God has truly filled my heart with inexpressibly great joy.

After beginning my new life in Christ, I began to grow and began conforming to the likeness of God. There was joy in discovering what it meant to know who I was in this world, and finding that, in Christ alone, I could be at peace and have gladness. I was not an accident! I was here by God's perfect design.

I never realized this blessed truth before I knew Jesus. I never knew I was thought of before the foundation of the world, or that I was in God's very mind. I humbly acknowledged the truth as expressed by the Apostle Paul:

> *Blessed be the God and Father of our Lord Jesus Christ, who hath blessed us with all spiritual blessings in heavenly places in Christ: According as he hath chosen us in him before the foundation of the world, that we should be holy and without blame before him in love: Having predestinated us unto the adoption of children by Jesus Christ to himself, according to the good pleasure of his will, To the praise of the glory of his grace, wherein he hath made us accepted in the beloved. In whom we*

have redemption through his blood, the forgiveness of sins, according to the riches of his grace.

[Ephesians 1:3-7. KJV]

God's presence in life is what we humans—the only part of God's creation for which Christ died—are always searching for, even before we realize it. Thus, leading others in and through Him will help them find what it is they want and are searching for in life.

Blaise Pascal, the renowned French philosopher from the 17th century, is credited with giving this description of our search,

> There is a God-shaped vacuum in the heart of every man which cannot be filled by any created thing, but only by God, the Creator, made known through Jesus.

The heart of mankind yearns for that void inside to be filled. We thirst for the One Who can produce the contentment, satisfaction, and longing that cannot be claimed or known until Jesus, God's Son, is invited to take residence in a repentant human's heart. Only in Him can life begin anew.

When Jesus filled my God-shaped vacuum, I was given hope for the very first time in my life. I would have been very happy to know that God cared about me before I turned 20 years old. Two decades of my physical life passed while I remained ignorant of that life-changing fact; but then some people cared enough about a fellow human being to share the Gospel with me, and when I realized I needed a Savior.

The conscious act on my part of responding to the drawing of the Holy Spirit and inviting Jesus in to reside in my heart, filled my empty void as nothing else had ever filled it. No experience, no chasing after illusive goals, no ideal situation or occupation had -- or ever would -- fill it. When Jesus invaded my life, life—past, present, future and eternal—took on new meaning and worthwhile purpose.

> *For God so loved the world, that He gave His only begotten Son, that whosoever believeth in Him should not perish, but have everlasting life.*
>
> [John 3:16. KJV]

In this single verse, the personal void all of us experience without Christ is and will be filled as we individually believe and comprehend that we are loved with a Love which will not let us go. The Creator God loves each of us so much He gave His only Son to pay the price for every sin ever committed—the gift of forgiveness for those willing to exchange their futile way of life for the Savior's perfect plan for life in its fullest sense.

Any loving parents can vouch for the amount of love they feel for their children, and can equally vouch with absolute certainty that they could never give their child's life in payment for the vilest of sinners of this world.

But in this verse we see that is exactly what God did with His only Son's work on the cross. We are also assured He doesn't want us to die, since He on the cross He conquered death, which will be the last enemy to be put under His feet. Moreover, He takes away our greatest fear, the fear of death, because He gives us life everlasting. Indeed, life's biggest issues are addressed in John 3:16: e,g., belonging and love, blame and guilt, life and death.

God so loved the world.... And God desires for us to feel confident in our abilities to lead others in this world to Him. This is possible if we humbly, but confidently, understand we are secure in Christ. A shaky, needy, uncertain, ashamed or doubtful person makes for a poor leader. Instead of being able to lead, that person needs to be led!

I am convinced that it is not religion that we need. The world has many religions. If merely "having" a religion was sufficient, surely mankind would not be in the condition it is in! What we need is a relationship with the Person Jesus Christ. He is the Gift, and He makes us unselfish. In Him, life begins, and Kingdom leadership can begin to shape us because Jesus's death and resurrection not only solve our personal problems and deals with all our sin, but also fill the void in our hearts and make possible his Kingdom on earth.

Kingdom leadership looks differently and has a different, richer focus than what is usually thought of as good leadership. In what way?

And the brother shall deliver up the brother to death, and the father the child: and the children shall rise up against their parents, and cause them to be put to death.

And ye shall be hated of all men for my name's sake: but he that endureth to the end shall be saved.

But when they persecute you in this city, flee ye into another: for verily I say unto you, Ye shall not have gone over the cities of Israel, till the Son of man be come.

The disciple is not above his master, nor the servant above his lord.

It is enough for the disciple that he be as his master, and the servant as his lord. If they have called the master of the house Beelzebub, how much more shall they call them of his household?

Fear them not therefore: for there is nothing covered, that shall not be revealed; and hid, that shall not be known.

What I tell you in darkness, that speak ye in light: and what ye hear in the ear, that preach ye upon the housetops.

[Matthew 10:21-27. KJV]

The same section reads similarly but perhaps with more clarity in the English Standard Version:

Brother will deliver brother over to death, and the father his child, and children will rise against parents and have them put to death, and you will be hated by all for My name's sake. But the one who endures to the end will be saved. When they persecute you in one town, flee to the next, for truly, I say to you, you will not have gone through all the towns of Israel before the Son of Man comes.

A disciple is not above his teacher, nor a servant above his master. It is enough for the disciple to be like his teacher, and the servant like his master. If they have called the master of the house Beelzebub, how much more will they malign those of his household.

So have no fear of them, for nothing is covered that will not be revealed, or hidden that will not be known. What I tell you in the dark, say in the light, and what you hear whispered, proclaim on the housetops.

Leadership does not typically call for the teacher or leader to be a servant. Jesus Christ is countercultural!

Jesus' exemplary life was one of contradiction of the status quo and what people thought was proper. He knew His message would not be popular to most in His day; therefore, His followers then—and still today—were warned to expect the same reactions as He received.

We will not be regarded as leaders in the "normal" sense of the word. But in the verses following the above Scripture section from Matthew, Jesus again instructs us not to be afraid. He cares about every detail concerning us:

And do not fear those who kill the body but cannot

kill the soul. Rather fear him who can destroy both soul and body in hell. Are not two sparrows sold for a penny? And not one of them will fall to the ground apart from your Father. But even the hairs of your head are all numbered.

[Matthew 10:28-30. ESV]

He can assure us of His care because He died for us when we didn't deserve it, and He has been through any hardship we could possibly encounter. He understands our fears and He travels life's paths with us all the way to heaven.

As Psalm 4:8 (cited earlier) assures us, we will "dwell in safety" because He is ever with us. That does not mean that our position of leadership will be without problems. Foes may oppose, friends may betray, life may feel like it's falling apart, things may be difficult, but He is always with and in us.

Jesus gives the ability to lead His way no matter what comes our way. He uses us as servant leaders who will lead in the countercultural way—that is, in the way of not being above teachers or earthly masters, but with servant hearts—not thinking we are better or higher in status because of our leadership position.

If we wonder why we are here in this world, we can do what I in fact did back in 1980, namely, to begin with God. No person is an accident. People need to know this. As stated in Ephesians 1:4, God thought about each of us individually, even before the foundation of the world. He still thinks about us. I would have been very happy to know that I was thought about and cared for by the One True God, and I never comprehended or could even believe it until He used other people to share His life-giving, life-changing Good News with me. Faith comes by hearing.

God not only fixed what was broken in me, but he called

me to join Him in fixing other broken things and people in his creation.

CHAPTER 2

Establish Credibility at Home

A good reputation and respect are worth much more than silver and gold.
[Proverbs 22:1]

When I began life in relationship with the Lord, my home life could only be described as difficult. As was mentioned before, there was an immediate, violent reaction to my new-found salvation through Jesus Christ. It seemed life around me was in chaos. Some family members suffered from depression, demonic attack, suicide attempts, self-maiming, and a myriad other problems.

My father, a hard-working farmer, did not understand his firstborn son's new beliefs. He claimed that I had betrayed and destroyed our family, causing him hardship, destruction of our family, and his loss of credibility in the community. My dad worked very hard to provide for the Lukos family, and now I—his 20 year-old son—was breaking with tradition and forsaking duties in my traditional position as a second father in the family.

Certain traditions were expected, and now it seemed that I was abandoning what were my rightful duties in the family, bringing shame and disgrace. When I also joined and identified with a small group of believers, my father felt shame as well as rage. He accused me angrily, "Saji, you have destroyed this family! Now who will marry my daughters?"

Finally, I was physically beaten and driven out of the family home. For two years I was away from home, but prayed constantly, asking God for my family members' salvation. I talked with God and told Him that I was happy, but would not be fully satisfied until my family came to the saving knowledge of Christ.

During this time of family exile, I took up residence in a city 60 kilometers from my home village. Throughout this time, I asked many Christians there to pray for the salvation of my family back home. Before trying to change the world; before changing anything or anybody, the cry of agony in my heart was the desire to go back to my village and to see my precious family come to know Christ and to see change happen in their hearts as it had in mine.

I prayed diligently *for* family, while acutely experiencing the pain of separation *from* family. I remained absolutely certain Christ could deliver my mother from her mental problems and my sister from demonic attacks. I knew the answer for many of our family's problems was in discovering the hope in Christ that I now knew.

Finally after two years, God burdened me to go back to my home village. Once there, I did not go straight to my parents' house, but respectfully went to see relatives who were neighbors and other relatives in the village.

Being the oldest son, our Indian culture made me the born leader of my family. Certain family leadership roles were expected of me, so when I seemingly forsook the traditions of the family for my "fanatical" new belief in a personal Savior, my leadership was questioned and even rejected. My family felt I had abandoned and rejected my expected traditional role. I had brought shame to our family; and my leadership role as oldest son was questioned, denied, and shunned.

These realizations almost broke my heart, but I had to follow my Savior and lead in a way that, at the time, was unacceptable to my family. I knew that my decision to take a path quite different than was culturally ordained by my family position could cost me the closest relationships I had enjoyed on this earth.

Prayer became even more impassioned as I cried out to God for the souls of my family members and my restoration into the family fold. I knew I had to be persistent in my prayers for my parents, brothers, and sisters. On my knees before the Lord, I fervently begged God for their salvation. I persisted until my prayers were answered.

Even though I had been kicked out of my home and had to live apart from my beloved family, I continued to communicate my love and care. I lived my Christian faith with persistence and, after a long period of time, my family eventually saw that many things in my life had changed in positive ways, changes due to the power of the Holy Spirit in me.

Relatives slowly began to receive me into their homes, but inevitably they would ask why I would do such a thing to bring such troubles to my family. They would remind me that I knew my own daddy's character, then ask why I would do such a thing as going against my daddy's wishes. Nobody in my family understood my faith.

Some of my Christian friends would come from the big city to hold evangelistic meetings, and I, desiring my mother's salvation and mental healing, would invite her saying, "Mother, please come. I love you. I did not abandon you." I asked my brothers and sisters to attend these meetings, as well.

In the Indian group- and family-oriented culture—which is not individualistic, as it so often is in the West—if the family leader trusts Christ and the family accepts that decision, then it is normal, easy even, for the rest of the family to also accept those beliefs. This is because of the important role of family leadership in Indian tradition.

As family members started attending the evangelistic meetings and some began to respond to the altar calls inviting them to trust in Jesus, I rejoiced in my prayers being answered. It was wonderful for me, since it was a matter of trust in the family leader. I took great care to show my love for my family, establishing the credibility that was so important.

Prayer over the course of many years eventually brought all of my family members into the Kingdom, and all serve the Lord in full-time ministry in some capacity today. As my focus of prayer, I made this Biblical principle my passion:

> *. . . but as for me and my house, we will serve the Lord.*
> [Joshua 24:15b. KJV]

All of my family eventually came to accept Jesus as Savior in their lives largely because—through Christ's enabling, not my own abilities, and the Spirit's drawing—I was able to patiently lead and witness to them. However, this was not an immediate result. It took many years before my last family member decided to follow Christ. Through God's grace, as they watched me walk according to Christ's leading, they saw living His way was the right way to live.

Depression was dispelled, demons were cast out, and Lukos family found true release and freedom in Christ.

My Spirit-led and diligent Christ-centered example showed my family a better way to live. I conducted myself in such a way that it attracted my family to the God I served, the God who had made my life so different in wonderful ways. When the hearts of my family members were softened by observing the way I lived, I was able to introduce and lead them to my

Savior. Then, I could disciple them and lead them into more maturity in Jesus.

Eventually my sisters married pastors, and a brother-in-law and brother joined me in the ministry I founded in India: Mission India (MI)—known as Reaching Indians Ministries International, or RIMI, in America.

Please do not be discouraged if family members do not know the Lord. They will come. The responsibility resting on each of us is to be an Andrew (John 1: 40-42). We must be our brother's keeper; our sister's keeper; our neighbor's keeper. Our responsibility is to be passionate about reaching our own family members, asking and crying and loving; doing everything within our human power, through God's enabling, to show them the love of God.

None of my family transformation would have happened without prayer and persistence to establish that pattern of credibility that finally allowed me to re-enter my family, mend relationships, and deal with them as a Godly leader. My life's example showed that following God worked. My Christian lifestyle proved I was honoring—not disrespecting—my father and the Indian tradition to care for my family. I led a respectful life of service to the Lord and to my family as well.

The God-given principles of credibility beginning at home which I honored and adopted are as follows:

- Pray with persistence
- Show love and care
- Establish credibility by how you live
- Evangelize and disciple
- Invite to join in ministry
- Experience transformation

Let's examine at each of these in greater depth.

Pray with Persistence

In the years that I prayed for my family, I never gave up petitioning, interceding, and making my requests known to God on my family's behalf. These were prayers of desperation as I went to battle on my knees for the souls of my loved ones.

Though I had been forcibly exiled from family, they were ever present in my prayers. After being kept away for a long season, God burdened my heart to return to my home village again—as hard as that might have been.

Even though danger was possible, even probable, under the circumstances of my leaving two years earlier, I obeyed God. In returning to my home village, I knew I faced possible additional rejection.

When prayers are answered and the results are obvious, even more credibility is established. Often the healing of loved ones, or other miraculous happenings are avenues to belief.

The facts that my mother was relieved of her suicidal depression and my sister was delivered from demonic attacks were clear testimony of what God was doing in the Lukos family and in me, in particular, as the result of prayer.

As God answered prayers and miracles unfolded, family members and other people of the community took notice. If such desperate situations were turned around, they thought that there must be something real in this new Christian faith that focused on a personal relationship with Jesus Christ, God's only Son.

In their past way of believing, knowing about God was all they knew. Now people began to see how belonging to Jesus and following the Bible and its precepts in relationship with Christ was a lifestyle that held promise and hope out to their troubled hearts. My season of prayer and persistence were coming to fruition.

Show Care and Love

Even though my family had beaten, threatened, and sent me away from home, I continued to care for my family. I loved them, continued to let them know I cared about them, and was genuinely concerned for their welfare. In the case my brother Regi, I helped him finish school and get a job.

While my presence was not welcomed in the family home, Regi told me of the concern there. It was said I was a bad influence, but my actions spoke otherwise. All during this time I was living a life of Christ-likeness by loving and caring for my parents and siblings.

Establish Credibility by How You Live

Once we become Christians, we can count on being observed. As we profess and begin to exhibits a new way of life, of being a new creation, people will be on guard to see what this change is all about. Even though our new lifestyle may be seemingly rejected by those watching us, the differences they see will be regarded with interest and curiosity.

The Christian lifestyle may even be hated— and Jesus tells us we can and should expect that. But when our lifestyle shows changes and we are diligent to make differences in our own lives and the world around us that are good and wholesome, it cannot help but draw the attention of those watching us. It may take time, and definitely patience, but it will speak volumes about how Jesus changes us through His Spirit.

How each of us conducts ourselves as a child of God will be testimony to our new lifestyle. The witness we give and the example we live out before others is extremely important. We may not be listened to, but count on this: We will be and are being watched.

Credibility is gained as our steadfastness testifies to changes observed in us are regarded as good. Differences will be noted, credibility will be established, and our conduct can draw others to desire to know the God we serve.

Evangelize and Disciple

When opportunities arise to share the "whys" of our Christian faith, we must take advantage of them. There may be a lapse of time between the seeing, the hearing, and the explanation, but people are watching, taking note of what they see. We will eventually be called upon to explain ourselves, especially as we establish credibility in our Christian life by our conduct and in sharing and witnessing, as we are led by the Spirit to do so.

With family, already established relationships allow for conversations when opportunities arise. But, at the same time, it may make it even more difficult because Satan enjoys attacking in the most vulnerable relationships where we care the most and are most emotionally invested.

It is absolutely necessary to share the Gospel. Faith comes by hearing. The way to salvation must be explained so others can make choices to know and love and serve Jesus. We also live our lives as an example and witness before others, but the time comes when we must give the testimony in spoken words.

Eventually we will be given the opportunity to ask others to make a choice to receive Christ's free gift of salvation, giving heart and life to Him. Their only alternative is to choose to reject the Truth.

If rejection happens, it does not signify an end to our responsibilities towards them. If rejection is their choice, simply continue praying, asking God for another future opportunity to share the Gospel, or for God to put someone else in their path who can share the Gospel.

When those close to us **do** in fact respond by accepting the gift of salvation and following Christ, it is important to get them involved and grounded in the Word and in fellowship with other believers. We should feel a responsibility to see them discipled and mentored in the true faith.

We should try to get them involved in a good Bible study and grace-based Christian fellowship where they can learn more about the God they have chosen to serve. Some of these studies are available through the Internet today. They will then begin to grow in knowledge of Jesus and what it means to truly follow Him and to become, as the Bible commands and as the Spirit leads,

> *. . . doers of the Word, and not hearers only.*
>
> [James 1:22a. KJV]

Invite to Join in Mission

In Christian circles, it is often said that our mission field begins at home. My own mission began at home as I agonized over the souls of my family members, and then was blessed to see them begin to come to Christ. God granted the desires of my heart and later allowed me to work alongside many of these same relatives and loved ones in the ministry in India and abroad.

Jesus started His own ministry with brothers. Who better to work alongside and minister alongside than those we love and trust most?

When family credibility is established to the point that they trust our words on the very destiny of their lives, and call upon the God of salvation for themselves, we should not ignore this! View them as what they are: natural partners and co-laborers in ministry.

There is a bond within the family and close friends that know Jesus that adds to the dimension of "closer than a brother." If we live out the principles of "Credibility at Home," we can lead our family and other loved ones into becoming a harvest of souls both at home as well as in the rest of the world. Family members can become ministry partners—and not only in personal mission, but also in the larger mission of reaching out and leading the peoples of this world to Christ.

There were times I felt how Joseph was treated by his family members, who sold into slavery to Egypt. Both he and I felt alone, misunderstood, and rejected by those whose words and actions hurt us most deeply. However, Joseph's ordeal helped save and bring blessing to his family and his people. His response to the very brothers who had wronged him was not one of anger or righteous indignation, but grace. His wonderful and gracious reaction to them provides an example we should follow:

> *. . . I am Joseph your brother, whom ye sold into Egypt. Now therefore, be not grieved, nor angry with yourselves, that ye sold me hither: for God did send me before you to preserve life.*
>
> [Genesis 45:4-5. KJV]

Yes, Joseph's brothers had caused him pain and years of exile, but he recognized that God used it for his good, as well as the good of his family. Years passed during which time Joseph could have developed bitterness, or fostered thoughts of retaliation, or fed a human desire for revenge.

Instead, Joseph chose to look at all of it through God's eyes. He recognized all he had endured and experience had led to a way to help his family and reestablish fraternal and paternal relationships at the same time. He regarded his trials and separation from his family as a blessing.

No revenge.

No retaliation.

Just God doing a work in Joseph's family for His own glory.

Slowly I began integrating family members into my ministry. After Regi came to know Christ, I took him to the big city to go to school. I rented a place for us to live in, and helped get him into construction work by getting him a part-time job with an acquaintance who was a civil engineer.

The transition of my brother from builder to partner made sense when I went to Nagpur to build the Mission India Bible College and Mercy Home. Regi went with me and helped develop the Nagpur land. He has proven, over the years, that he will, quite literally—because of our relationship as siblings and co-laborers with Christ—do anything for me in the Lord.

Regi works in the ministry and, as my brother and confidante, can be called on any time, day or night, to come to my aid. Laying the original groundwork to any relationship can be difficult but, in our case as physical and spiritual brothers, it has resulted in present and eternal benefits.

Here I would like to insert a caveat regarding the involvement of relatives in mission. In America's individualistic society, doing so can be regarded as nepotism. But, if handled carefully and undergirded with prayer, it can be and is often a good idea. Beloved, trusted family members make natural choices for ministry partners.

On the other hand, if it is all and only family members involved in the ministry or on the "inside" so to speak, then "outsiders" may feel inferior and threatened. So it is important to keep a balance.

In the group and family-oriented framework of society within India's culture, I am free to work closely with many of my family members. Because of the long-established and honored traditions of that particular cultural setting, family-working-with-family is not thought of as unusual or unhealthy.

However, while it is vital to be sensitive to cultural differences in whatever setting one works, the Lord can and will break down any cultural barriers if decisions are based solidly on prayerful consideration and on sensitivity to God's leading.

My siblings all eventually became believers, and I had the privilege to lead my grandfather to Jesus, as well. After eight years, my father also came to Christ; he was the last in my family to do so. After my dad became a fellow believer, God transformed him to become a wonderful Godly man who encouraged all his children in ministry for Jesus.

Today most of the family members are in mission field work because of my father. God transformed Dad's anger and hatred into a turn-round for our whole family.

In India's family culture it is natural to follow after the family leader; but in God's Kingdom, there are additional rewards of love and belonging both now and in eternity.

And now, we have reached the final principle of credibility beginning at home, which I have pursued since my own life was radically changed by Christ's work in me.

Transformation

I lost my father on July 23, 2013. I had received a call from my father who desperately wanted to see me. I was traveling in northern India, but God had allowed me to send Mony and Maryann to go stay in Kerala with my father near the end of his life.

Grandpa Lukos told Maryann he was so happy she was

there. I had no idea that my father was near death. I knew my father's heart was failing, but still thought he would live at least a few more years of life here on earth.

I arrived in Kerala on July 20, and had a couple of days to visit my father. On the morning of the 23rd, I was getting ready to leave for the airport to fly to Nagpur.

That morning, my father asked me, "What time are you leaving?"

I said, *"Around ten o'clock, Daddy."*

With that settled, my father went to get ready and take a bath before saying his goodbyes. He never came out again. His heart had quit in the bathroom, and he went home to be with the Lord.

I was glad I was able to be there at that time, but his death was a shock. I lost a father who had become—in such a transformation from his former attitude of many years before—a big support in ministry for all of our Lukos family.

I am grateful to God for his faithfulness and His extra measure of grace in transforming all of my family members to experience a new life in Christ. However, it is important for you to remember that although everyone in your family may not receive Christ as soon as or in the manner you expect, we are commanded to continue to pray for their salvation and continue to show our transformed life as an example.

CHAPTER 3
Identify Your Destiny

The highest destiny of the individual

is to serve rather than to rule.

– Albert Einstein

The first year after I became a Christian, I was still completing my schooling while simultaneously being involved in evangelistic meetings. I had moved from the dormitory where I was staying to live with two evangelists who brought me to the faith. I did not have one-on-one mentoring to grow in my faith, but I was always with these missionaries: attending Bible studies, various meetings, and doing evangelism, all the while continuing my studies.

These two men also arranged for tutorial sessions for me with a boy in the nearby village. I would leave school around half past four o'clock and would walk three miles to a house at a rubber plantation to teach. This was how I discovered my love for teaching.

The missionaries were the ones who opened a door to my future, helping me with the opportunity to teach and to realize more of my gifts outside of business and accounting. Following my tutoring of the boy, I received invitations to homes to tutor more students.

During that year, I also completed my Bachelor of Arts degree in business, went to the capital of my state and became involved in a Bible church. Again, I did not have one-on-one discipling. But in India it is common for new Christians to spend time with the pastor of a church just as Jesus spent time with His disciples. Doing this enabled me to see how the pastor lived and what he did. This was my "mentoring" in ministry.

Today I do the same with my RIMI and MI staff members. I keep them near when I am around, despite having limited time with my travels between India and the United States. We study together, look at Bible passages together, and talk about issues in the ministry. This was the pattern of how I learned the Christian walk from the missionaries with whom I lived and the pastor who mentored me.

Often, even when I travel, I will have one of my staff or others involved in the ministries travel along with me. As a companion in traveling, they can see how I work and interact with others.

This enables them to learn by observing, lets them help alongside and perhaps discover their own gifts as they try new things and observe various situations in ministry. They see me preaching, dealing with people, doing fund-raising, teaching, and visiting with anyone who are or will become involved in ministry in India or elsewhere in some capacity.

All of God's creation possess unique qualities and gifts. Each of us is given a special place in His creation, meaning, that we all play a part in His Kingdom that only we—as unique individuals—can play.

We must realize and accept this truth in order to foster a desire to find out what God has called us to do. God created each of us in a special way with special abilities to contribute a part in the big picture of His Kingdom. God indeed has a special plan for each life he created—a plan He desires to be fulfilled by the person upon whom He bestowed it—no one else. To identify our life's destiny, let's consider some key questions within several imperatives.

Identify Your Calling

Question: What is God calling you to "do" in life?
Question: How exactly has He strategically equipped you to further His Kingdom?
Question: Have you ever asked yourself if there is something God wants you to do for His Kingdom that no one else can or will do?
Question: What is it?
Question: How do you find out?

Recently, I noticed an item on Facebook that spoke to the calling you have on your life:

> *The things you are passionate about are not random. They are your calling.*
>
> [Posted by: Fabienne Fredrickson]

My own calling was being developed during the time I was with my friends and pastor as well as listening to visiting evangelists. I was being discipled and challenged in my walk with Jesus Christ, and was all the while identifying my strengths that could be used in Kingdom ministry.

My encounter with God during the preaching of Ravi Zacharias (which will be described later in this chapter) drew me more to knowing, worshipping, and ultimately understanding what my calling is. God developed me through circumstances and Divine appointments.

Dr. Zacharias' view of worship speaks to what I was going through at this time of identifying my calling:

> *Worship is a posture of life that takes as its primary purpose the understanding of what it really means to love and revere God.*
>
> [From: Zacharias 2 in 1: Jesus Among Other Gods (and) Deliver Us from Evil]

In loving, worshipping, and revering God, He will guide us to our unique calling in and service in His Kingdom.

Identify Your Gifting

Question: What gifts do you have that can be used for Kingdom work?

Question: How has God equipped you specifically to carry out your place in His global plan?

Too often, our too-quick, too-easy response is, "I have no talents," but we learn in I Corinthians 12 that the body of Christ which is made up of believers from all nations, is comprised of believers that have all kinds of talents and gifts. This chapter of Paul's Epistle indicates we all have a purpose to fulfill in the body.

It is obviously true that the head is more visible than the little toe, but that does not make the little toe unnecessary. Think about stubbing a toe. It makes the whole body aware of a hurt. A little splinter in any part of the body can cause an infection that affects the whole. Hit a finger with a hammer, and the throbbing will keep the rest of the body awake at night.

In other words, each part will affect the rest of the parts and the whole body.

Question: So, how do you find out what part you are to play in this body of believers?

God gives the gift or gifts, and it is up to us to find out what it is. More than likely we will be gifted in an area in which we feel capable, and acting on that capability will help us identify our gifts. By seeking (or welcoming) advice from spiritually mature and trustworthy people, we gain insight from their observations.

The counsel of Godly leaders may help in discerning gifting. Sometimes we might discover through thorough investigation; at other times our gift is a surprise to us as we learn that we are gifted in ways never recognized by us before.

Writing to the church at Ephesus, Paul addresses what that phenomenon might look like:

> *And to know the love of Christ, which passeth knowledge that ye might be filled with all the fullness of God. Now unto Him that is able to do exceeding abundantly above all that we ask or think, according to the power that worketh in us.*
>
> [Ephesians 3:19-20. KJV]

That gift may "come out of nowhere" by God's leading each of us into something that will show us strengths we can (and are expected to) use for His Kingdom. In that case, it is "above all that we ask or think." Whatever the gift is, we are to seek to discover it and then to use it for God's glory and purpose in His Kingdom.

Just as I Corinthians tells us that the body of Christ has "many members," we can deduce that even in many parts, God designed it to work together in harmony and unity. One body part does not try to fight off or destroy another part in a healthy situation. We are all part of one Body. We each have one unique-to-us purpose, and whatever our gifting is, we are called to bring glory to God, with every part working in unity with the rest.

If we fail to discover and use our gifting, we are being less than we are intended to be. Not only that, but we are diminishing what can be accomplished for the Kingdom. God loves us too much to let that happen, if we are seeking Him and His will for our lives. And when we discover and use our gifting, we are doing all we are intended to, and we are multiplying accomplishments for the Kingdom—to God be the glory!

Identify Your Purpose

As Christians, it's not about us, it's all about Jesus.

Therefore, let's ponder these pointed and personal questions:

Question: **Who** is the *purpose* all about?

Question: How are you "wired"?

Question: Are you absolutely convinced that you can do nothing without the working and leading of Jesus and His Spirit in your life?

Question: Is your life a testimony that points to Him?

Question: Is your sole purpose in life to make Him known, loved and served?

Because it is not about the proverbial "me," but it's all about Jesus. And we learn that when we let Him live through us, we get our own real and personal needs and desires fulfilled as well.

Question: So, is this your primary purpose—to make Him known?

The psalmist gives us a remarkable picture of where we come from and what our ultimate purpose is in life. Look at how God views His creation:

> *For You created my inmost being; You knit me together in my mother's womb. I praise You because I am fearfully and wonderfully made; Your works are wonderful, I know that full well. My frame was not hidden from You when I was made in the secret place, when I was woven together in the depths of the earth. Your eyes saw my unformed body; all the days* ***ordained*** *for me were written in Your book before one of them came to be.*
>
> [Psalm 139: 13-16. NIV]

In these encouraging verses, we see we can rely on the fact that God knew about us even before we were born, and that we were uniquely made to fit into His plan. He "ordained" our days—meaning He planned them out, and He knows where He is leading us.

He "knit" us together—meaning He wired each of us uniquely according to His pattern for our lives. He knows our "frame"—everything about us, and the patterns for our lives were all in His book before we were even born!

When we say, "God has a plan for my life," we could not be more accurate. He formed us and wired us for a specific task, a specific niche that only we individually, but by His enabling, can fill.

Rick Warren, the well-known pastor and author of The Purpose Driven Life, lists five purposes which speak to identifying our ultimate destiny. Let's consider them, briefly . . .

Purpose 1: *We Were Planned for God's Pleasure*

Our first purpose is to offer real worship, to give pleasure to God. Do that by really worshipping Him, by wholeheartedly giving Him all praise that He is worthy of, and by acknowledging that He is God Almighty, the One to whom we can absolutely bow in adoration.

Our worship truly does give God pleasure. We constantly need to ask ourselves, "Am I worshipping God as if it is for Him alone?

Purpose 2: *We Were Formed for God's Family*

Our second purpose is to enjoy real fellowship. We can grow through enjoying Christian fellowship with others of like belief. We can find strength in fellowshipping with others who enjoy God as we do.

When we become part of God's family, we find we have like passions, and feel affirmed to express them in freedom. We can have accountability and partnership with those who become brothers and sisters—if not through blood, by Christ's shed blood. We can be fed when we worship with others of like mind, study with others, get together, and edify one another.

Fellowship is vital food of a spiritual kind. You and I need it for spiritual nourishment, and we find that in the family of God.

> *A man that hath friends must shew himself friendly: and there is a friend that sticketh closer than a brother.*
> [Proverbs18:24. KJV]

Purpose 3: *We were Created to Become Like Christ*

Our third purpose is to learn real discipleship. Reading God's Word and spending time with Him in prayer, adoration, and meditation helps us begin to become more and more like Christ.

As we develop in this love relationship—a two-way relationship, with Him loving us and us loving Him all the more as we learn more and more of who He is—we can learn real discipleship. We follow and emulate who He is because we develop a love relationship with Him.

We want to be like the One we adore. We desire to spend time with Him. We want to please Him by our life's actions. It enables us to be able disciples and to mentor others, as we look for others who can pour examples into our own lives, keeping us accountable.

It becomes a cycle of loving and living like Him, of Him enabling us to love others, and then of Him receiving the praises from us that are due Him, along with adoration and praise from those we disciple.

Jesus had a band of men around Him called disciples. If we are created to be like Him, making Him known and emulating Him, we too will learn real discipleship.

Purpose 4: *We Were Shaped for Serving God*

Our fourth purpose is to practice real ministry. Ministry is only occupation unless God is in it.

Real ministry is serving God in the capacity we were created to fulfill.

Real ministry is not doing tasks for a church or Christian organization.

Real ministry is making God's glory known. We see that throughout the Bible in verses like this:

> *For ye are bought with a price: therefore glorify God in your body, and in your spirit which are God's.*
>
> [I Corinthians 6:20. KJV]

John Piper writes about bringing glory to God in all we do:

> The Bible is crystal-clear: God created us for His glory. Thus says the Lord, 'Bring my sons from afar and my daughters from the end of the earth, everyone who is called by My name, whom I created for My glory' [Isaiah 43:6-7]. Life is wasted when we do not live for the glory of God. And I mean all of life. It is all for his glory. That is why the Bible gets down into the details of eating and drinking. 'Whether you eat or drink, or whatever

> you do, do all to the glory of God' [I Corinthians 10:31]. We waste our lives when we do not weave God into our eating and drinking and every other part by enjoying and displaying him.
>
> [From: *Don't Waste Your Life*]

Purpose 5: *We Were Made for Mission*

Our fifth purpose is to live out real evangelism. God equipped each of us for a purpose: to know, love and serve Him and make Him known, bringing glory to Him.

Our mission in life should be evidenced by a desire to see others know the glory of following Jesus Christ. When we are able to let others see who He really is, to be able to reflect His glory, we are able to share that glory with those we encounter daily.

As we make His glory known, we can live out real evangelism. our mission becomes wanting to make Him known; His fame and glory revealed to all.

The words of Dr. Tony Evans (to which I have added italics at the end) emphasize this point:

> God will often take you from where you are to where He wants you to be at what can be called a "Divine intersection". This is the time and situation in your life where your gifts, skills, passion, experience, and personality merge together into either the revealing of, or carrying out of, your destiny.
>
> What many of us try to do in our lives is rush ahead to this intersection, not realizing the importance of God's perfect timing. Until your divine intersection comes, God is preparing you for that moment—for the people, tasks, and purposes ahead. And He is also preparing your

destiny, the people and places involved, just for you. This is similar to what He did in Canaan when the Israelites entered the Promised Land. God had already provided for the Israelites because the Canaanites had dug the wells, cultivated the land, and built the communities in that land.

Friend, if you learn anything at all from Scripture about reaching your destiny—learn this: Don't go searching for your destiny. Go searching for your God.
[From: *Destiny*]

Slowly, through in my life's many experiences--not only being away from family as happened initially—I was being prepared to serve and lead. God put me in positions of servant leadership and prepared me through hard experiences and sufferings. These difficulties built Godly character and developed skills in me which would first help my family and eventually others.

Leaders are born in crises and in tough situations when someone has to step forward to direct people forward. I was willing to do this. But all the while I was being molded into what God planned for me to be.

I had no say in my birth-order position as firstborn son, but it put me in a leadership position as younger siblings grew up and needed counsel and aid. While attending university, the tutoring I did house-to-house for students before going to my own classes kept me developing and fine-tuning my teaching skills.

Tutoring also enabled me to pay my rent, and begin to have siblings come live with me. This income allowed me to care for them and provide for furthering their education, to have money for food, and to hone my innate teaching skills. This I did out of necessity, but in teaching in order to raise funds to survive, I found something I was gifted in and loved.

Evenings and weekends, I preached and held small evangelistic meetings. I got involved assisting, as time allowed, in various ways at services at the church I attended. I listened intently to, and would respond to, visiting preachers' and evangelists' altar calls for those who would surrender their lives in service to God.

God was refining His call on my life. He was establishing my destiny.

I clearly remember the call Dr. Ravi Zacharias gave after preaching to a crowd of thousands on the Old Testament book of Habakkuk. He challenged the crowd, seeking for anyone who was willing to serve God. I raised my hand with conviction that this was my calling.

Whatever I asked of God, He granted as the desires of my heart. One by one, members of my family began to know, love and serve God. I was living a life of peace and joy. Earlier I had started an accounting school, eventually teaching over 200 students a year. But all of this was preparation for God's shaping and honing my eventual full-time ministry and His developing of my leadership qualities.

I was learning about myself and found strengths surfacing that God had planted within me. Eventually, God laid on my heart a burden for people, especially those of my home country, India, and throughout Southeast Asia.

In an example of irony and Godly providence, my parents, early on, had dedicated their firstborn son—me!—to the priesthood. When I was four-years old and my sister was two, we were playing outside of our home. Not knowing any better, we picked and ate some very poisonous mushrooms. We both had to be hospitalized for many days and almost died.

Because of this incident, our parents—grateful that two

of their children had not died—had dedicated me to the priesthood. I believe God's hand was upon me from those early days—protecting, guiding, and shaping me for eventual ministry. Many of life's experiences were difficult, but by His grace and Spirit I began to open seek God, and thus began the process of recognizing that calling upon my life.

When I immigrated to New York at the age of 28 years old, I had a good job, but I was restless. I kept asking myself, "Am I, a young Indian immigrant, going to live like other immigrants?"

I could look at fellow immigrants and see that many were consumed only with making money, often sending it back to India to help their families. I, too, wanted to help my family, but other things were on my heart. It was at this point in my life that this particular Scriptural imperative became key:

> *Love not the world, neither the things that are in the world. If any man love the world, the love of the Father is not in him. For all that is in the world, the lust of the flesh, and the lust of the eyes, and the pride of life, is not of the Father, but is of the world. And the world passeth away, and the lust thereof: but he that doeth the will of God abideth forever.*
>
> [I John 2:15-17. KJV]

These verses indicate a removal of affections from what the world has to offer to the life that God has to offer. This means a life of servant-hood, not self-hood. Temporal things of the world pale in comparison to God's eternal forever.

This Scripture was also the impetus that led me to go to seminary and dedicate myself to full-time ministry for the purpose of serving God and the people put in my pathway. After consulting with Dr Ravi Zacharias, who already had had a profound impact on my life, it was clear I should go to Trinity

Evangelical Divinity School (TEDS) in Deerfield, Illinois.

TEDS was a school that would help shape and form me for my ultimate calling: to give my life to bring glory to my Savior. The school's mission statement encourage me; it is "... existing to serve the church of the Living God by equipping servants for the work of the Gospel of Christ worldwide." This confirmed what was already in my heart.

I desired above all to take the Gospel back to my homeland. My heart was especially drawn to the plight of orphans and marginalized people of India and Southeast Asia. My whole life up to this point had been preparing me to do ministry in those areas that spoke to my heart.

I had many people who had poured blessings into my life in many ways to help fulfill my destiny. History gives us many examples of people who were changed and directed into their calings because of how God allowed life to shape them.

A prominent example of this is Mahatma Gandhi, who, although not a believer, was another individual from India who was shaped for his destiny by what he experienced in life. He became the primary leader for India when declaring independence from British rule in 1947.

Gandhi was able to employ nonviolent civil disobedience through social protest to win civil rights for many marginalized people. He was born into the merchant class and trained as a lawyer, beginning his studies in India and completing them in London. It was during his time in England that he became involved in causes that strengthened his leadership role.

Ghandi went on to practice law in South Africa after a brief return to India. There, he was able to develop his skills in practicing law while working among the Indian expatiates. He became involved in their cause and was jailed, but he steadfastly refused to employ violent means of protest and change.

In 1915 Mahatma returned to India to organize lower class people against the oppression of unfair taxes and caste discrimination. He later led campaigns against poverty, and for rights among women and lower caste people. Again he was jailed, but those accumulated experiences gave him the ability to nonviolently lead the country to independence later on.

He became world-famous for his peaceful demonstrations against the practices that kept so many Indians enslaved within the caste system. All of these accomplishments and involvements helped shape Mahatma Gandhi to be the man whose name is synonymous with the independence of India. His life experiences also trained him to put himself selflessly in the line of danger in order to secure the rights of others. All the while he lived a life of simple self-sacrifice and led peaceful demonstrations that finally spoke to the world's conscience, pressuring the British to grant India's self-rule.

Assassination claimed Gandhi in 1948, but the world never forgot his example of giving self for country. His experiences with rejection and oppression had shaped him to influence and inspire many others to fight against rejection and oppression in their own circumstances.

Two other examples of people who were shaped by their destinies are Martin Luther King Jr., and Mother Teresa. Both spent time in India—one to learn, the other to devote her entire life to the poor of India.

Martin Luther King Jr. was born in the South during turbulent times in the history of the United States. He was born into a pastor's family in 1929. As such, he enjoyed a certain status in the Black community at that time in history.

From the very beginning, he was to follow in his father's footsteps and become a pastor. His father even renamed him. At birth, he was named Michael, but his father renamed him after the great instigator of the Reformation, Martin Luther. Martin Luther had been a reformer, stepping outside his role as catholic priest in order to counteract the religious status quo of his day.

In keeping with his name change, Martin Luther King Jr. also became a pastor who stepped out of his normal role of pastoring a church to become involved in the American Civil Rights Movement. It was not easy growing up in the South. There was much civil unrest because of the discrimination against his people.

King knew there were separate waiting rooms, drinking fountains, and parks for Blacks. He knew some were not free to vote without retribution in some areas of the South. All in all, Blacks were not treated the same as whites, and it was unfair. He saw and felt the impact of the times, and he wanted to bring about reform but without violence.

His early life formed in him ideals for equality while guiding him on the pathway his life would take him. In his famous "I Have a Dream" speech, delivered 28 August 1963, at the Lincoln Memorial, Washington DC, he asked only that his children be given the same opportunities as anyone else:

> I have a dream that my four little children will one day live in a nation where they will not be judged by the color of their skin but by the content of their character.

That's all he really wanted: for all people be treated with dignity and equality.

King had been taught well by his devout parents, so even though he saw things as unfair he did not believe in violence.

He therefore reacted to the mistreatment and prejudice of the time with nonviolent civil disobedience, and he crafted speeches that spoke volumes to multitudes. Quiet "sit ins" and marches with only signage giving his message, were his ways of getting a point across, and the point was: "Treat African Americans the same as you would like to be treated." He lived the Golden Rule.

Martin Luther King Jr. refused to fight with fists and weapons, but chose to use careful words and quiet disobedience of unfair laws. He was arrested and thrown into jail many times, pelted with rotten fruit, spit upon, and mistreated in many ways. But his nonviolent approach and response to injustices against him personally spoke to the country. Attitudes were changed. The cause was eventually joined by others who thought the laws were unjust.

King did not have it in him to react with violence, even in the face of violent behavior toward him and his fellow demonstrators. He once said,

> "I have decided to stick to love . . . Hate is too great a burden to bear."
>
> [*"Where Do We Go From Here?"* Southern Christian Leadership Conference, Atlanta GA, August 16, 1967]

It was well known that Martin Luther King Jr. had studied Gandhi's philosophy. Although also ending tragically in assassination, his life had spoken for his cause in ways that would outlive him.

It had been his destiny, from the time of his birth and his renaming, to change his world by fighting without violence. His Christian beliefs shaped his destiny, and he reacted by giving his life to further justice for all people of any color

Mother Teresa was a contemporary of Martin Luther King Jr. She was born in 1910 in Eastern Europe and felt called to become nun by the age of 12. She became a nun at the age of 18, leaving home never to see her birth family again. A devout believer, she often publically stated her desire was to care for:

> ". . . the hungry, the naked, the homeless, the crippled, the blind, the lepers, all those people who feel unwanted, unloved, uncared for throughout society, people that have become a burden to society and are shunned by everyone."
>
> --Mother Teresa

She went to India after learning English in Ireland, believing her destiny was to teach and began teaching in Calcutta (Kolkata) India in 1948. As she travelled daily to the school where she taught, she could not help but see the homeless on the streets there.

It was during these daily journeys into the inner city that she received what she called her "call within a call," and that was to form her own religious order, the Missionaries of Charity. Her daily journey was impacting her heart, and her heart was confirming her destiny to minister to those she was passing, seeing, and feeling compassion towards. And so it was that she left the order she was in at the time, and began to minister to the poorest of the poor in Calcutta, with little more than basic medical training.

In the beginning, she had many difficulties: no money, no food, etc.; and she had to go out begging herself for food and supplies for her work. But those earlier trips into Calcutta, and her having to resort to the indignity of lack, of begging, was shaping her into the woman of God she was meant to be. Mother Teresa ministered in Calcutta for the rest of her life.

She also became a world-renowned champion of the destitute and won the Nobel Peace Prize, the US Presidential Medal of Freedom, and multiple universal awards. Although world leaders and royalty admired her, but her heart was with the poor, loving people of all faiths, serving Jesus, fulfilling her destiny.

> Mother Teresa frequently gave this response to two questions about her calling: *"Who am I? What am I supposed to do in life?"*
>
> By blood, I am Albanian. By citizenship, an Indian. By faith, I am a Catholic nun. As to my calling, I belong to the world. As to my heart, it belongs entirely to the heart of Jesus.

We must not blame anyone for our circumstances. We are in charge of only what God gives us. We can respectfully ask our Creator, "God, what are You doing in my life?" Our duty is to identify our destiny from where we are —the place where God has put us. We are where we are for a reason; think of it as part of God's divine plan.

Unless we rely on God, we may accuse others for our place in life. We also will want to find the reasons things that have happened, and it is only human nature to blame another for what, in our eyes, went wrong.

In my quest, I didn't have much time to place blame. Many days began with beatings. These rose out of my father's ignorance before my father came to know Jesus. I had often thought I should have been born into someone else's house. Many times I did not appreciate what was happening to me. But I now firmly believe that if I had not gone through the exact experiences I went through, I would still be in India not doing anything for the Kingdom today.

So try not to blame your background. Ask God to show you His purposes in putting you where you are.

CHAPTER 4

Pray Specifically

Bold prayers honor God, and God honors bold prayers. God isn't offended by your biggest dreams or boldest prayers. He is offended by anything less. If your prayers aren't impossible to you, they are insulting to God.

– Mark Batterson

Praying specific requests. This is praying with expectation, and it is key to accomplishing what God has in store for you. When you pray specifically, you will see results.

Prayer coupled with fasting increases the intensity of praying. It seems to bring focus and purpose to the obedient act of praying and communing with God.

The prayer known as The Lord's Prayer [Matthew 6:9-13] contains the troubling phrase: "Thy will be done." It means that God's people put their own desires or wills aside and put those under God's authority. It means God's people trust Him and His love to do what is best.

How can this be? Because God knows all about us and has His beloved's best interests in His mind when He performs His will.

If we pray expecting God's will, we are yielding *our* will to *His* will to accomplish His Kingdom's purpose on earth, as

He has in heaven. We are believing that God will work for "the good of those who love Him" [Romans 8:28].

Another key phrase is: "They Kingdom come." If we are to be Kingdom leaders, we need to seek first seek his Kingdom in our life and ministry. This allows us to lead as God's representatives in Kingdom.

David Platt, author and pastor whose name and ministry are often linked in Christian circles to *radical* thinking and action, talks about following God's will. He says the question of following the will of God is "quite possibly the most commonly asked question in Christianity today." He believes Christians fail in identifying the absolute, primary purpose of being a follower of Christ, and that is to be "fishers of men" [Matthew 4:19].

In other words, we must first and foremost present the Gospel of Jesus Christ. That is God's will for us. We can take many different paths and there are many different occupations. But in whatever place we find ourselves, it is the will of God for us to present His Gospel to those who are perishing without it.

We should pray specifically about how we can arrive at a place where we can best use what God has given us to reach others for Christ. Quoting David Platt:

> We operate as if God's will were lost . . . With good intentions, we try hard to use various methods to find God's will. But what if God's will was never intended to be found? In fact, what if it was never hidden from us in the first place?
>
> . . . And what if searching for God's will like this actually misses the entire point of what it means to be a disciple of Jesus? Consider how discipleship transforms not only our minds and emotions, but also our wills. You

and I have seen that when we come to Christ, we die to ourselves. To return to Paul's words, each of us says as a Christian, "I have been crucified with Christ and I no longer live, but Christ lives in me." As followers of Jesus, our lives are subsumed in His life, and our ways are totally surrendered to his will.

[From: Follow Me: *A Call to Die. a Call to Live*]

When we look at what God's will is for us in that light, it becomes clear that the career path is secondary to the primary goal of being an instrument of the Gospel, loving God joyfully, and leading people to a knowledge of Him. As Godly leaders, we may expect answers from God that are our good, not necessarily what we desire.

Thankfully, He places us on a path where we can enjoy Him. He makes serving Him a joy and not a burden. God doesn't promise us forever-blue skies here on earth, but He does promise to be with us during our stormy skies—or any kind of skies.

In his well-named classic book of devotional readings, My Utmost for His Highest, Oswald Chambers reminds us:

We have to pray with our eyes on God, not on the difficulties.

Difficulties will and do come. We can--and should—expect them while we are still here on this earth. But the triune God will be with us through every trial, as well as every joy. His Word promises it!

And this is the confidence that we have in Him, that, if we ask any thing according to His will, He heareth us: and if we know that He hears us, whatsoever we ask, we know that we have the petitions that we desired of Him.

[I John 5:14-15. KJV]

The secret is in two words: "His will." Do we trust God enough to do what is best for us when we pray? After all, we are to pray for God's will, not our own. John RW Stott puts it this way:

> Prayer is not a convenient device for imposing our will on God, or for bending His will to ours, but the prescribed way of subordinating our will to His. It is by prayer that we seek God's will, embrace it, and align ourselves with it. Every true prayer is a variation on the theme "Your will be done."
>
> *[Tyndale New Testament Commentaries: The Epistles of John.]*

I have seen many, many prayers answered. I have learned to pray specifically always with the self-exhortation, "Thy will be done," but it is clearly God's will that His people trust in Him, trust in His love.

It is God's will that people everywhere come to know Jesus Christ and His salvation. His desire—His will—is for people to get healed and be delivered from their afflictions and fears. It is God's will that the poor are fed, clothed, and cared for. It is God's will that those mired in false religions come to trust in His truth. It is God's will that marginalized people be valued.

God's will is always what is best. For everyone.

I wrestled with God for the souls of my family, and was able to see God answer my prayers. My success (humanly speaking; God's blessing, in the Divine perspective) in praying for my family, and those who came to the evangelistic services, as well as other relatives and loved ones, gave me the boldness to pray for other things in God's Kingdom.

When God answered prayers in miraculous ways, I had even more confidence to pray more and more. I saw lives of family members and others transformed, especially that of my sister Lissy.

As a young teen, Lissy had suffered from demonic attacks. She had been possessed, and often held the family in fear as she made demonic demands in the voice of her long dead grandmother and made threats for favors or the consequences of death of family members.

God released Lissy from all of that and she gave her heart to Jesus. In fact, when she moved to the city to live with me and our brother Regi, she now had the spirit of love and peace, and became the acting "mother" of our household: a Christian household.

When not managing our home, Lissy became a prayer warrior and fasted often. She also rallied her family members to pray, as she continues to do today. She was a tower of prayerful strength against spiritual attacks. I knew this was due to God's transformation from chaos in our family home into our home of prayer and caring for one another.

My father had accused me of ruining the marriage possibilities for my sisters due to my new-found Christian faith. This was difficult to hear, yet I had not forsaken my traditional responsibilities and I began to pray for the marriage of my sister Lissy. I asked God for a Godly man who would make his sister a loving husband.

The answer? She married Pastor P.D. Joseph, and is a faithful wife who continues to be a prayer warrior. Her husband is a strong national leader and a powerful speaker (and singer) for MI throughout India.

My Lukos brothers and sisters each, by 1983, came to accept Christ and follow Him in obedience by being baptized. They also evangelizing in and beyond their own locale.

We were conducting a service in front of the home of one of our father's relatives when it started to rain. Knowing continued rain would call for cancelling the service, and wanting to show the power of God to display the glory of a God who has power over the elements, the Lukos siblings prayed for God to reveal Himself to the many people who had gathered there to hear God's Word. Miraculously, the rain stopped, causing many unbelievers to see the power of the living God. Many heard the Word of God that night as a result of God's glory displayed.

This answer to prayer had another positive outcome: I was recognized by my family and villagers as a powerful speaker. Once again, God used circumstances to mold my leadership capabilities as family leader, evangelist, and powerful speaker.

The beginning of Mission India in Nagpur was truly a humble beginning. I met with godly leaders who were identified on my earlier trips to India and I established a board of directors to operate Mission India.

After this, we still needed land to build my dream of a Bible school to train people to plant churches throughout India, and on which to build a Mercy Home to care for children needing a safe place. There was no natural way to get enough land to start the ministry I was convinced God wanted me to start.

I began fervent petitions to God, praying without doubting that God would answer; and He answered way beyond anything I had dreamed of. God provided a plot of land and we were able to purchase it in 1999. Later, $5,000 was donated to us; and Mission India was able to construct a foundation for the large building which is now the center for all work in India. God also provided a separate office space for the headquarters in the nearby city of Wadi.

Prayer is of paramount importance to me and to RIMI and MI; in fact, everything revolves around prayer. Connecting with God is how we operate. There are regular individual, family, ministry, and staff prayer times. Prayer happens. Often. I pray because it is my lifeline, and I have witnessed it working, time and time again. It is the foundation, the backbone of everything.

For the remainder of this chapter, I will elaborate on seven essential points on prayer:

1. Prayer pleases God.
2. Prayer changes things.
3. Prayer works with faith.
4. Prayer is needed for others.
5. Prayer is needed with others.
6. Prayer with fasting.
7. Prayer like Daniel's.

Prayer Pleases God

John Piper, via his online devotional, Solid Joys, quotes the prophet Isaiah in answering the question, "What kind of prayer pleases God?"

> *This is the one I esteem: he who is humble and contrite in spirit, and trembles at My Word.*
>
> [Isaiah 66:2b. NIV]

With that in mind, Piper continues:

> I conclude from this that the first mark of the upright, whose prayers are a delight to God, is that they tremble at God's Word. These are the people to whom the Lord will look. So the prayer of the upright that delights God comes from a heart that at first feels precarious in the presence of God. It trembles at the hearing of God's

Word, because it feels so far from God's ideal and so vulnerable to his judgment and so helpless and so sorry for its failings.

"A humble and contrite spirit" would be the sinner realizing a need for God, and trembling in God's presence as a prayer of confession is voiced. That would also be one so desperate for God that it would be impossible to turn elsewhere.

We can offer prayers that are all about ourselves and our various needs and concerns. But unless we pray out of hearts that acknowledge God as holy and just and worthy of our trembling, are we not just voicing words that only our ears hear?

God wants to meet, in prayer, with people who are "contrite in spirit," just as David was when he said:

> *The sacrifice acceptable to God is a broken spirit; a broken and contrite heart, O God, Thou wilt not despise.*
> [Psalm 51:17. RSV]

With a need apparent in our very spirits, God loves to hear from us. He wants to hear from us, and promises in His Word to answer our prayers.

People tend to want to hear God's answer to prayer only if it agrees with the prayer they prayed and answer they envision. But often God answers prayer in ways we have not thought of, and it is always a better answer than what we wanted or expected.

Prayer pleases God because it is through prayer that we can have that two-way conversation with Him. People often fail to do the "two-way." We want to list all our requests, pleas and petitions, but we fail to listen and meditate on the One to Whom we are speaking.

Nevertheless, God always loves to hear from us. He wants to hear from us. He delights in the times we deliberately spend with Him. He also likes to speak us.

The Puritans had a saying, "Pray until you pray." Prayer should be and can be our lifeline but, to make it that, we must make sure the lifeline is connected both ways: to Him and from Him. A day of "praying without ceasing" can be any day that we continually think on God, and commune with Him as we go about the day's tasks.

He knows what we are doing and what we are in need of, but when we pray to Him continuously throughout our day, He is communicating with us in a way He loves. We don't need a bench or an altar or even a quiet place, we just need to consistently be in the mindset of talking to Him, aloud or silently in our hearts, and He will hear us and be pleased.

Of course, there are times for the altar and the closet of prayer, but praying without ceasing cannot always have those places. Sometimes the place maybe at the kitchen sink, or in the midst of a board meeting. It matters not what the location. What matters is the heart's location, and that must be focused on Him. We please God when we talk to Him. After all, that is what prayer is: talking to God.

American evangelist, pastor, educator, and writer R.A. Torrey said,

> I must pray, pray, pray. I must put all my energy and all my heart into prayer. Whatever else I do, I just pray.
>
> [From: *How to Pray*]

Torrey further states,

> Those persons who know the deep peace of God, the unfathomable peace that passeth all understanding, are

always men and women of much prayer.

None of us can survive successfully—and in the peace which only God can give us—without prayer.

Prayer Changes Things

Most of us have seen this adage printed on a wall poster or plaque, a bumper-sticker or greeting card, or even a coffee cup or T-shirt:

PRAYER CHANGES THINGS

But the saying is more than religious sentiment to display or wear. Prayer does change "things."

First of all, prayer changes us—from the heart on out! Prayer touches God's heart. Sincere prayer shows God we adore Him enough to talk to Him and to yield ourselves to Him in prayer with Him, not just to Him.

In Oswald Chambers' daily devotional previously cited, he says:

> Prayer is not a normal part of the life of the natural man. We hear it said that a person's life will suffer if he doesn't pray, but I question that. What will suffer is the life of the Son of God in him, which is nourished not by food, but by prayer.
>
> When a person is born again from above, the life of the Son of God is born in him, and he can either starve or nourish that life. Prayer is the way that the life of God is nourished.
>
> Our common ideas regarding prayer are not found in the New Testament. We look upon prayer simply as a means of getting things for ourselves, but the Biblical purpose of prayer is that we may get to know God Himself.

> . . . To say that "prayer changes things" is not as close to the truth as saying, "Prayer changes me and then I change things."
>
> God has established things so that, on the basis of redemption, prayer changes the way a person looks at things. Prayer is not [always] a matter of changing things externally, but one of working miracles in a person's inner nature.
>
> [From: *My Utmost for His Highest*]

If we take Chambers' words to heart, we will pray that God first deals with our hearts and, as other things start to come to mind to pray for, we will know we are in communion with Him, our heart is right before Him, and we can sincerely pray "Your will be done."

The problem is that often prayer is thought of as the last line of defense instead of the front line. Corrie ten Boom, who endured the horrific Nazi concentration camps during World War II, is widely credited as the originator of a penetrating question, "Is prayer your steering wheel or your spare tire?"

Perhaps best known for authoring the autobiographical *The Hiding Place*, Corrie ten Boom practiced what she proclaimed to vast audiences:

> Don't pray when you feel like it. Have an appointment with the Lord and keep it. A man is powerful on his knees.

It is the norm to go to God in prayer when we are at the end of what we can do. We forget where our power comes from. When we are being self-sufficient, we are not depending on God. We are really telling Him that we will go to Him after we finish what we can do on our own. We put Him in second place, right behind ourselves.

And how does that work for us?

That's a rhetorical question!

We well know how that works! Instead, why not let God be our first source for all we ask or of all we think? Then, and only then, will we really see "things" change.

Prayer with Faith

Here's a challenge: We are to ask in prayer, in faith, believing with sincerity and humility that God hears our prayers. Psalmist David was aware of that kind of prayer. Throughout the Psalms he cries out to the Lord in prayer. One of many examples is when he pleaded:

> *Lord, hear my prayer, listen to my cry for mercy; in your faithfulness and righteousness come to my relief.*
>
> [Psalm 143:1. NIV]

The verse refers to God's faithfulness in answer to our pleas for mercy. But James 5:15 refers to our faithfulness as well:

> *And the prayer offered in faith will make the sick person well; the Lord will raise them up. If they have sinned, they will be forgiven.*
>
> [James 5:15. NIV]

God is faithful. No question about that. But we must also show faith, even if our faith is only the size of a mustard seed [Matthew 17:20]. Prayers with even that small amount of faith will, as the passage states, move mountains.

That passage also states that our faith will cause nothing to be impossible. Possibilities expand when we exercise faith in God.

Prayer for Others

Praying for others is what a committed Christian does. God gives us a heart of concern for our fellow human beings and all that concerns them when we draw near to the God who hears our prayers.

The verse following the one listed above gives instruction:

> *Confess your faults one to another, and pray one for another, that ye may be healed. The effectual fervent prayer of a righteous man availeth much.*
>
> [James 5:16. KJV]

The whole James 5 passage makes it unequivocally clear that it is important how we deal with our fellow workers, and others all around us. Prayer for another will do very little if we are treating them in a way unpleasing to God.

So our attitude in prayer and for those we pray for should be that we are to be clean before the Lord and to spend time in prayer for those we encounter.

Prayer with Others

We can have sweet fellowship with God and with others when we pray together. Prayer is dealt with many times in the Bible (in the King James Version, the word "pray" alone is mentioned 313 times) and we can assume that it is important to God, to our relationship with Him and with others.

Prayer is encountering a living, active, working God, so it cannot be taken lightly. Gathering fellow believers together for prayer about shared passions and ministry is not only advisable and healthy, but it is a lifeline. We cannot live without it—spiritually or corporately.

> *For where two or three are gathered together in My*

name, there am I in the midst of them.

[Matthew 18:20. KJV]

That verse uses the word "together" and promises God's presence when we do so. It is fairly safe to say that we cannot fight and disagree in unpleasant ways with others if we pray with them. Praying with others cements relationships in many ways; and even if there is disagreement, it would be able to be handled in an agreeable fashion.

Prayer with Fasting

If we want to put focus in our prayers, we should pray with fasting. This is not easy, but it is a small, small sacrifice to sharpen our senses to the purpose for prayer.

Fasting is mentioned in both the Old and New Testaments. As Campus Crusade (being only one of many credible supporters of the discipline of fasting) proclaims, fasting was a discipline that was expected in Bible-times. In the Old Testament, Moses fasted and prayed.

In the New Testament, Jesus fasted and prayed. In Matthew 6:16, our Lord said, "When you fast," not "if you fast" (emphasis added).

In that same passage, He also cautions that we are to have the right attitude, or the results will be less than we desire and more about the spectacle we make of fasting.

Another Old Testament passage on fasting speaks of humility:

. . . I wore sackcloth; I afflicted myself with fasting; I prayed with head bowed on my chest.

[Psalm 35:13. ESV]

Ezra recalled the fasting for the preparation of renewed

worship when the temple in Jerusalem was opened to worship once again. The attitude of those fasting and prayer was one of humility and penitence.

> *I proclaimed a fast, so that we might humble ourselves before our God.*
>
> [Ezra 8:21a. NIV]

These two passages show us that fasting is not to be undertaken lightly or with an "entitled" attitude. Fasting required humble hearts open to God.

Fasting transforms a time of prayer into a more deliberate, meaningful dynamic, one marked by God's expectation for humility, worship, and results.

Prayer like Daniel's

Daniel was a man of prayer. When hearing his name, we often think of the Biblical account of the lion's den. Indeed, the sixth chapter of the book of Daniel tells how this Godly young man escaped the jaws of the hungry lions by spending the night in prayer. His prayer, though, was witnessed by three, and possibly four, kings who ruled over Babylon where he was exiled. They saw him survive a night in the flames of a fiery furnace, as well as watching (and possibly hearing) him pray.

Prayer also stood Daniel in good stead as he saw visions, interpreted dreams, and prophesied the future. An unusual man, Daniel kept up his daily practice of praying even in a foreign land, and that earned the scorn and hatred of those who saw his presence and promotion as a threat to themselves and their positions.

Many times throughout the book of Daniel, we read of Daniel praying for God's mercy, revelation, deliverance, and supply for daily needs. Ezekiel calls Daniel as "righteous"

[Ezekiel 14:14, 20] and refers to uses him as one of the examples of who would be saved:

> *. . . even if these three men—Noah, Daniel and Job—were in it, they could save only themselves by their righteousness, declares the Sovereign Lord.*
>
> *. . . as surely as I live, declares the Sovereign Lord, even if Noah, Daniel and Job were in it, they could save neither son nor daughter. They would save only themselves by their righteousness.*
>
> *[Ezekiel 14:14, 20. NIV]*

Deductions can be made that Daniel had a prayer-pattern which we can live by, and it is a pattern of much prayer, even in the face of opposition—especially in the face of opposition.

CHAPTER 5

Dream a God-Sized Vision

God is up to something big when he plants his dreams in our hearts, and it's so much bigger than us.
– Michael Hyatt

Just as we cannot out-give God, we cannot out-vision God. He expects us to think big. Why? Because He is a big God: the Creator of the universe.

Vision, however necessary it is to leadership, is not always easy to articulate. *In Follow Me*, David Platt writes that we are not to look at buildings or programs but instead to look at people. You and I might know in our minds what God's vision for us is, and feel it in our hearts, and believe in it with passion, but how do we put it into practice and let others know so they too can share in it?

To be great servant-leaders who will lead others in a manner that realizes God's purposes enacted in the world, we have to actually lead—to get others to share the vision so that they, too, can act upon it. God does not need anyone: He is more than capable of doing anything He wants, but He chooses to work through His people because He loves us and desires a mutual relationship with each of us in which we absolutely, wholly depend upon Him as our partner and reason for ministry.

That means we can simplify ministry and not make it so hard; just focus on people! The rest will follow. I did not start with a Bible School, Mercy Home, classrooms, offices, and a hospital. I started with people. I started with a vision, a dream.

When we have God's vision, we have something bigger than ourselves, something that only God has the power to equip us to work alongside Him. So, as it is in India, the number of those who need to hear the Gospel staggers the mind, but I am convinced that to reach the multitudes, we must train people who can speak to multitudes.

In a May 2014 gathering of the staff in the RIMI office near Chicago, people who had learned and worked under my style of leadership brainstormed about God's vision for those in ministry. They compiled this list of vision "musts"—

- Vision needs to be big.
- Vision needs to be clear.
- Vison needs to be passionate. It is the fuel to keep workers encouraged to continue.
- Vision needs to be communicated.
- Vision needs to persevere. There is a time element. We are faced with limited time. Urgency is essential.
- Vision needs endurance.

In keeping these rudimentary principles as my central focus for what God had directed me to do, my vision was and continues to be to reach all the states of India and beyond. I have encountered opposition, which is to be expected when one is engaged in warfare on a battlefield.

Sheer numbers can be discouraging with India's 2,256 people groups and 2,033 of those groups still unreached with the Gospel, as reported by the Joshua Project (www.joshuaproject.net). That translates into almost 1.18 out of 1.27 billion souls yet to be reached.

The task is daunting, but a God-sized vision is a vision that trusts in a big, all-powerful God. Militants and governments have tried to halt Christian work, especially in some regions; but knowing that it is the vision God laid on my heart keeps me and those involved in MI pressing forward.

MI workers have been persecuted at times, but many MI workers and church planters count that a privilege. In fact, many who encounter what Americans would consider persecution do not even call it persecution.

In 2013, a friend of RIMI visited Karnataka and the MI Bible School in Gulbarga. During interviews, some of the students gave remarkable answers to the question, "Have you encountered persecution because of your faith?" Some pastors did not consider beatings, being exiled from family, or being run out of their villages, to be persecution. One commented that they had not been killed, so they did not call it persecution!

Recently an MI Bible School was shut down by a local government. Prayers are that it will eventually be reopened, but this just shows that the opposition is strong. God is stronger, and my God-given dream is to establish Bible Schools to train church planting pastors throughout each state in India and beyond --and with each Bible school to have a Mercy Home where orphans and the poorest of the poor are fed, clothed, and educated.

For the remainder of this chapter, I will expand upon six component-questions which I deem vital to my vision and by which I evaluate it:

1. Is it from God?
2. Is every facet for His glory?
3. Will it result in transformation?
4. Is it based on the greatness of God?
5. Is it presented to others with clarity?
6. Do I communicate it with passion?

From God

A vision must clearly be from God—not just what we see, but what God envisions. We must try to think as big as He does. Humanly that is impossible, but we serve a big God who desires to work through us. That takes a yielding of self and our will so that He can accomplish what He knows is best, in His love for us.

His plan for us is His way of fulfilling His destiny in us and showing His love in our lives. It is up to us to make sure it is clearly from God. That will come sometimes through much hard work agonizing in prayer. The old phrase "praying through" is appropriate here.

If we spend enough time with Him to lay everything out before Him, the time spent with Him helps us start to discern what He is responding back to us. Only then can we map out the course He has set, aligning our wills to His purpose.

Search out every personal plan to see that it aligns with His. He is bigger than we can ever imagine, so if we impose our own ideas on His vision, we are limiting God's best for us.

Even though the vision has to be relevant to the culture, it cannot come from the values of the culture, but it must come from the teachings of God's word (Romans 12:1-3).

For His Glory

God desires for His fame to be known among all peoples. He created us for His glory. As John Piper says in his tract *Quest for Joy*,

> God made us to magnify His greatness—the way telescopes magnify stars. He created us to put His goodness and truth and beauty and wisdom and justice on display. The greatest display of God's glory comes from deep delight in all that He is. This means that God gets the praise and we get the pleasure. God created us so

that He is most glorified in us when we are most satisfied in Him.

. . . Bring my sons from afar and my daughters from the ends of the earth—everyone who is called by My name, whom I created for My glory . . .

[Isaiah 43:6b-7. NIV]

A holy God is all about glory, and He wants the peoples of this world to proclaim His glory.

. . . give unto the Lord, glory and strength. Give unto the Lord the glory due to His name; Worship the Lord in the beauty of holiness.

[Psalm 29:1-2. NKJV]

This psalm clearly tells us that God is glorious, strong, and holy. And He deserves, is "due," our praise and worship acknowledging who He is—beautifully holy and glorious.

On this earth, there are few things to which we can ascribe such awe-inspiring attributes, but in the Bible it is the theme: to make His glory known among all nations. In fact, in the Old Testament, the word "glory" is often synonymous with God. So God is not only glorious, He is glory itself. We are to make that glory known, making Him known.

Look at Jesus' words in John's Gospel where we see His words with His Father about the glory that was theirs:

I in them, and Thou in Me, that they may be made perfect in one; and that the world may know that Thou hast sent Me, and hast loved them, as Thou hast loved Me. Father, I will that they also, whom Thou hast given Me, be with Me where I am; that they may behold My glory, which Thou hast given Me: for Thou lovedst Me before the foundation of the world.

[John 17:23-24. KJV]

Jonathan Edwards, a theologian and fiery preacher in the 1700s, expressed his thoughts on God's glory on many occasions, but one of his most succinct and opted repeated is:

> "God's purpose for my life was that I have a passion for God's glory and that I have a passion for my joy in that glory, and that these two are one passion."

As people with that passion, may we also be able to say with conviction, as Edwards did:

> "Resolved: I will live for God. Resolved: If no one else does, I will still live for God."

For Transformation (of People and Society)

It is extremely difficult to impact individuals for God's glory because people are such a poor reflection of His glory. But it is even more difficult to be the catalyst that affects society as a whole for good.

Transformation of society begins within each individual. We must be aligned with God's plan in order to be a part of what He plans for the rest of the world. God's Word is clear: We need an inner renewal:

> *Do not conform to the pattern of this world, but be transformed by the renewing of your mind. Then you will be able to test and approve what God's will is—His good, pleasing and perfect will.*
>
> [Romans 12:1. NIV]

This "renewing of your mind" is only the beginning. As the oft-quoted Charles Stanley (television preacher, pastor, author, and founder of *In Touch* ministries) states it:

> Renewing the mind is a little like refinishing furniture. It is a two-stage process. It involves taking of

the old and replacing it with the new. The old is the lies you have learned to tell or were taught by those around you; it is the attitudes and ideas that have become a part of your thinking but do not reflect reality. The new is the truth. To renew your mind is to involve yourself in the process of allowing God to bring to the surface the lies you have mistakenly accepted and replace them with truth. To the degree that you do this, your behavior will be transformed.

My personal transformation made me grateful that I have been privileged to be part of God's vision that has impacted many places in India and around the world. I firmly believe that once personal transformation takes place, the vision God then gives us for His Kingdom must center on the transformation of people and society.

A person who can help transform society can do it either positively or negatively. To be an agent to touch society in ways that changes it positively takes a vision as big as the God who gives it. He alone is able to see such a change take place.

The late Adrian Rogers—television preacher, pastor, Bible teacher, author, and Christian leader who was known for his evangelistic zeal and uncompromising commitment to the Word of God—proclaimed and believed,

> The same Jesus who turned water into wine can transform your home, your life, your family, and your future. He is still in the miracle-working business, and His business is the business of transformation.

God wants to change people from sinners to saints, and society from users and exploiters to givers and servers. The choice is ours individually. Each of us can be a person who:

- brings about Kingdom work to any person or any place, and
- is an instrument in God's hands to affect the society in which they live, interact and have an impact.

God can multiply our efforts to completely transform our homes, our communities, our world. We give . . . and He causes that small bud of an act of giving to blossom into something far beyond what we could ever imagine.

I have a big dream, but it has gone farther than I imagined, because it was from God. The work for the Kingdom still continues to expand and grow and touch many souls. I continue to pray for millions . . . even, billions!

Based on the Greatness of God

God, who is the Creator King, can accomplish big things from the visions of small people. This is true because Kingdom accomplishments are based on how great God is, not how great people are.

In and of ourselves, we are nothing in comparison to God, but He loves each of us— personally —and He chose each of us—individually—before the foundation of the world. That makes us worthy to partake in His purpose and work in this earth when His vision becomes our vision.

I am in awe of God's greatness, and am very aware that knowing that is foundational to any ministry. God does not work in small ways. He is able to accomplish great things, but He uses—and needs—those of us who are committed to His will as His hands and feet to accomplish it.

Clarity of Vision

Jonathan Swift, the 18th century satirist and essayist, defined vision this way: "Vision is the art of seeing things invisible."

A vision is not merely something you or I desire and can achieve. If it is to change lives and impact our world, it must be what God wants and empowers. Life-changing vision must clearly be from God. Too often people think, "I want it so badly, God must surely want it, too."

There are avenues necessary to explore that will aid us in clarifying vision:

- prayer
- fasting
- listening
- God laying it on our hearts over a period of time
- studying God's Word, and
- the counsel of people we trust and know are mature in their own faith walk with Christ.

Our vision must be clear because people we minister to and those with whom we work will not understand it if it is not clear to us. In order to communicate what is to be done, we must be clear on what God wants.

Everything in the world must become as nothing in comparison to where God leads. Where He wants us to go, and what He wants us to do must be so clear we know exactly where to go and what He desires. We are involved in His work, which clearly lasts forever, so we must think beyond now and begin to think in terms of work that endures forever.

Communicate with Passion

When we are clear on what our vision from God is, we will need to be able to communicate it so as to be able to pass it on to others. If we are abiding in Christ, we will have a passion to pass it on. We cannot get that passion by reading books (even this one!) or newspapers and magazines. That passion comes by knowing God and abiding in Him and loving Him in a two-way love relationship.

According to Revelation 5:9, we anticipate a time when there will be people from every tribe and tongue and people and nation will have had the opportunity to hear the message of the Kingdom. That is why the message must be passed on effectively—so everyone can understand the truth of the Gospel. This calls us not only to communicate our vision of Kingdom here on earth, but to love the people God wants to see come to Him. It is, simply, a matter of life and death—eternally.

> *Do not love the world or anything in the world. If anyone loves the world, the love of the Father is not in him. For everything in the world—the cravings of sinful man, the lust of his eyes and the boasting of what he has and does—comes not from the Father but from the world. The world and its desires pass away, but the man who does the will of God lives forever.*
>
> [I John 2:15-17. NIV]

Long before those words were penned, God inspired the writer of Proverbs to warn us, regarding the absence of vision:

> *Where there is no vision, the people perish.*
>
> [Proverbs 29:18. KJV]

With all humility, I didn't have a 32-acre piece of land in Nagpur, but I had a dream. I saw the land. I saw the buildings. When I didn't have the land, I still saw.

I saw Moody Bible College. I saw Wheaton. I saw Trinity.

All I saw helped me to dream. Coming to American helped me dream big. I learned the history of this vast country, America, and how the history was formed by ordinary people like Harvard University's benefactor, who gave funds to help found the famous university.

Few precise details are known about John Harvard. There was no photography in the 1600s, and he was a Puritan minister, so there is also no known portrait of him. What little is known about Harvard (who lived 1607-1638 AD) is reflected in this statement from the college's brochure,

John Harvard was a Godly gentleman and a lover of learning.

[From: "New England's First Fruits"]

That Harvard was instrumental in founding one of the world's most famous learning institutions is a miracle. Most Puritan ministers had little money, and he was relatively unknown except for his crowning accomplishment of being Harvard's first benefactor, earning the honor of the institution being named for him.

On his deathbed, John Harvard bestowed half of his inherited estate to the college being founded by the Massachusetts Bay Colony. His legacy, small by today's standards, has affected countless people.

Wheaton College's founder was another "ordinary" man who would not be known except for the college he founded. Jonathan Blanchard, an abolitionist and pastor, would have been considered a failure by some in his day. He left his place of study in New York because he was rejected for being a member of an antislavery society, and was forced out of a college presidency after the Civil War.

Despite this, he went on to found Wheaton and presided as its president for 22 years until his son, Charles, succeeded him. Wheaton College and Jonathan Blanchard are known and respected today because the college promotes strong faith and academic excellence.

Early immigrants to America represented all kinds of people who gave up all in a place they knew to make their home in a new country. They sought a chance to found a nation on the principles of God.

Many of these visionaries (those who, like Jonathan Swift, saw things invisible) came as missionaries to the Native Americans who were here. Doing so cost many their lives, through illness or martyrdom.

The Swedish Baptists, coming to America from the familiarity of their Scandinavian homeland, began arriving in the 1700s. Many had left home because they could not gather for Bible study and were being arrested and jailed for their beliefs.

These Swedish immigrants founded many churches and learning institutions, some of which were the forerunners of the Evangelical Free Church in America, and Bethel University in Minnesota. In Deerfield, Illinois, Trinity International University (TEDS) was originally founded as a Bible course, which grew into a university.

TEDS' original roots arose out of the Swedish Evangelical Free Church, the Norwegian-Danish Free Church, and the Evangelical Free Church. Having begun in Minneapolis, the school moved to the Chicago area in 1949 and became Trinity Seminary and Bible College, eventually Trinity College and Trinity Evangelical Divinity School. As mentioned earlier, this where I received my seminary training and degree.

In looking at all this history of what had transpired in American history, I can only be amazed at the Godly influences that had brought about some of the great movements of faith and education in the United States. I was burdened further, beyond America, because there are only 350 million people in the USA. In India there are over 1.2 billion souls.

I'm so thankful I learned to dream big in America where a rich history of large Christian movements was instigated by ordinary people. I knew I needed to dream big if I was to reach my home country for the Kingdom of God. Just how those significant Christian movements had been founded for and by the greatness of God, not just the abundance of American money, that impacted me. This showed me what could happen in a land where God was honored by its founding fathers.

It has all happened because God is so big. The vision is different for different people and different places, and I am astounded by the enormity of God's work and by what huge things have happened in history to further that work, by individuals:

- There was only one Dwight L Moody, impacting his world for God in his time; and
- We've seen only one Billy Graham doing God's work, in God's way.

Both of these men accomplished big things with God. There have been many such "small," relatively unknown people who have accomplished much.

Why do I mention this? Because there is only one Saji Lukos and only one you. That is the ultimate reason we need to ask God how He has wired each of us. As we listen and hear His answer, we must trust Him to give us the vision for our place in His big plan for the whole world to be won for His Kingdom.

If we don't know that our vision is from God, it will be hard to carry it out and to keep it going, let alone assist in making it into something big that only God could grow. I understand the sense of floundering! A lot weighed on my heart as I made plans for my own ministry.

I credit many people for their sacrificial help in helping get me established to carry out my vision, and to continue to carry it out. My confidence in an unshakable God Who gave and guides my vision is what has sustained me in the midst of many conflicts and trials along the way. Knowing God implanted the vision in me allows me to ever be able to press forward in my work for His Kingdom.

My relationship with my Lord and Savior, and the grace of God and my understanding of that grace, the mercy of God, my understanding of who God is, and my continuing to learn about God, along with the ever present need in India—all these keep me going and growing.

I frequently retell the story of Mother Teresa going to India to teach, and getting a "call within the call" born out of the need she saw daily. That was what established Mother Teresa on her path to her destiny. To this day, the need she saw and addressed is both present and prevalent in India. It is the often overwhelming (from human perspective) and very real need which helps me maintain my vision of the work with RIMI and MI.

When I was seeking to understand and "flesh out" my vision explore and develop and ministry opportunities, I spent six months reading only Nehemiah and the story of his vision for his people. Respected pastor, author, educator, and radio preacher Charles Swindoll wrote in his article, "Seven Building Blocks for Leaders," that the Old Testament book of Nehemiah is a "storehouse of leadership insights."

In searching out my abilities, I used Swindoll's thoughts and the principles found in Nehemiah to propel me. I took a trip throughout India from Kerala to Kashmir with the goal of soaking in the scenes of India, and viewing the country and people's needs first-hand. For those six months, I told no one of my prayer: that God would reveal to me what I was supposed to do.

I traveled in trains and buses and cars. I explored the land. I talked to people. People I already knew in India were excited and happy to see me. They saw the man who had returned to his home after he had immigrated, but I didn't share why I was there this time. Thus, I traveled from the South near my home to places I had never been in the North—all for the purpose to ask God to move me as He had moved Nehemiah.

I could have stayed in Kerala where I was comfortable and at home, but my six months of travel helped me identify Nagpur as a central launching site for a large work throughout all of India. Vison comes, but not always without work. I needed to travel. Why? Because I needed to immerse myself in India in order to:

- see the need;
- develop a burden; and,
- identify the brokenness.

With these factors central in my mind and weighing on my heart, I could begin a mission with the vision God was establishing all the while I traveled.

Since then God has sustained the vision because I have seen the change, the life transformations. Especially encouraging were the changes I saw in my own family. That helped me develop the passion to see the same thing happen to others. I praise God for all that happened, and give God the glory for that confidence in my vision that God has placed on my heart – to help save India and other nations for the Lord.

CHAPTER 6

Faithful in the Little Things

There will always be more people willing to do "great" things for God than there are people willing to do the little things. The race to be a leader is crowded, but the field is wide open for those willing to be servants.

– Rick Warren

I've been told I don't know the meaning of the word "lazy"! If so, it is because I have worked hard my whole life and was never allowed to shirk my work or duties. My father was a hard taskmaster, but I do not resent that in any way. I credit him with teaching me the value of hard work, and have never forgotten that lesson.

I helped in the rice fields, and helped to collect coconuts and mangos. Crops take a lot of water in the hot climate of India, so he had to haul water. Today water is piped into my family home, but in the days of my childhood, our home had no running water or nearby piping. When I came home from school, I had to draw water from our family well. It seemed as though there was always water to carry!

Later, when I was kicked out of my family home because of my new-faith in Christ alone, I had to get up early to work to get food. I would walk miles to give children tutorials, and I did it well because all of my students got great marks in their studies. I would be teaching by 6:00 AM, and then go to school myself. As has been mentioned earlier, while working on my master's degree, I started an accounting school.

Always, I worked. God helped me to work hard, from early morning until late at night. My needs were always provided, and I always had work to do. I didn't know it at the time, but God was already preparing me for my future in ministry. It is the same for anyone who is being prepared for the future. The future may be unknown, but God uses the present to prepare His people for what lies ahead, whatever it is.

> *Whatever you do, work at it with all your heart, as working for the Lord, not for men, since you know that you will receive an inheritance from the Lord as a reward. It is the Lord Christ you are serving.*
>
> [Colossians 3:23-24. NIV]

A Kingdom-style leader is faithful in little things to accomplish the big things. Wherever God places us is the place where we are to serve Him and make His glory known.

I have adopted five principles of faithful leadership by which I live and attempt to model for others:

1. Be faithful where God has placed me.
2. View the past as preparation for the future.
3. Remember: God is faithful.
4. Give my best.
5. Accept that my ultimate reward comes from the Lord.

Be Faithful Where God Has Placed You

God is faithful, and He has placed each of us where He wants us in preparation for the future. We must never serve God only half-heartedly, but serve Him willingly and with a whole heart.

It does not matter where God has placed us in life, or what we are doing as long as we are in the place God wants us whether we are . . .

- single and living alone: that's great.
- a plant manager in charge of thousands, or a stay-at-home mom of six: that's great
- a corporate executive, that, too, is great.

Get the idea? *Wherever, whoever* we are, we each must make sure it is where we need to be to serve God to the utmost. There is nothing more important than what we are doing if it is God's will.

Whether "in charge" of one or over multitudes, we are equally responsible to God. Ultimately He is in charge, and we need to be responsible in and for all that He has entrusted to us individually.

In the parable of the talents that Jesus shared with His disciples as recorded in Matthew 25:14-29, the man who was entrusted with ten talents was just as responsible as the one given one talent. It wasn't because the one-talent recipient had only one that he was condemned; it was because he had done nothing with what he had been given.

Each of us are responsible for our *little* or *much*. Jesus' parable indicates that, as leaders—whether responsible for little or much, over a few or many—we are to care for what and who He allows us to lead.

Kittie L. Suffield was a singer, pianist, and wife of the evangelist who was preaching when George Beverly Shea (the soloist most often associated with Billy Graham's Crusades) was converted. In 1924, Mrs. Suffield wrote a poem—which was later set to music—which speaks volumes into the truth of being faithful in little things:

Little Is Much

In the harvest field now ripened
There's a work for all to do;
Hark! The voice of God is calling,
To the harvest calling you.

Refrain: Little is much when God is in it!
Labor not for wealth or fame;
There's a crown, and you can win it,
If you go in Jesus' name.

In the mad rush of the broad way,
In the hurry and the strife,
Tell of Jesus' love and mercy,
Give to them the Word of Life.

Does the place you're called to labor
Seem so small and little known?
It is great if God is in it,
And He'll not forget His own.

Are you laid aside from service,
Body worn from toil and care?
You can still be in the battle,
In the sacred place of prayer.

When the conflict here is ended
And our race on earth is run,
He will say, if we are faithful,
"Welcome home, My child—well done!"

[Public Domain]

Scripture supports these truths in Jesus' parable of the mustard seed [Matthew 13], in His feeding of the multitudes [John 6; Matthew 14], in the story of Gideon [Judges 7], just to cite a few examples. Whichever illustration is considered, the point is clear: God expects that whatever He entrusts to us should be used to the utmost of our abilities. If there is an increase with our little, we are to acknowledge the increase comes from Him.

View the Past as Preparation for the Future

My whole life has been preparation for what I am doing today. My father was a hard worker and taskmaster who expected the same from his children, especially me—his oldest son. The chores he assigned me when I was young taught me that hard work is a way of life as well as a preparation for my future.

Learning to work hard early in life made me what some consider indefatigable today. As mentioned before, I shouldered the Indian culture's traditional role for oldest-son as family leader, making it natural for me to lead in all types of situations as head of MI and RIMI.

In every role I was assigned or born into, I strove to be faithful to learn my lessons well. Those lessons have well served me throughout my life and ministry. Every little detail has contributed to what has been accomplished. To God be the glory, honor, and praise!

In fact, the ministry we do in our God-sized vision is also preparation for our future work in the new creation (Luke 19:11-27). In the new creation, we will serve the Lord in his Kingdom in all eternity with no pressure of time and no sin to struggle against.

Remember: God Is Faithful

When I immigrated to the United States from India at the age of 28, I arrived in New York to start my new life with a total of $3,000. I needed transportation, and was able to purchase a car for $2,800. That left me with $200 to begin a new life.

I immediately needed the $200 for rent, which left me with virtually nothing with which to get started. Then, as I felt God urging me to get schooling for ministry, I moved on to Trinity International University (TIU) in Deerfield, Illinois. During my whole time there, I sent money back to my parents and siblings. How could I do that? God faithfully provided for me and helped me meet my responsibilities every step of the way.

At one point, I held down four jobs: security, cleaning a church, a retail store clerk, and driving a school bus. Later, I taught business classes at TIU. All of this seems a heavy load while doing ministry and taking additional schooling. I consider none of it a burden, as it was God's provision to me, and it was what God had been teaching me in the past. When I started RIMI, I was living and operating my ministry on $500 a month. Such small beginnings for a ministry now reaching throughout all of India and beyond; it can only be a result of God's multiplication.

Below are three examples of Godly models that help me be faithful to a God Who is ever faithful.

The first example is King Saul and one that taught me to be careful. King Saul—an impressive man according to Biblical accounts—became petty and jealous, ending up in all-out, unfaithful rebellion against God when he became "big." He was a monarch but, in his prideful disobedience, he forgot God in the end.

The second example is Billy Graham who came from humble beginnings: milking cows in the early morning and working for Youth for Christ. Then, God called him out of that organization to become a youth pastor. He promised God that whenever he preached, he would always give an invitation to accept Christ. The farm boy became a respected evangelist who spoke to people all over the world, including to presidents and to world leaders.

A third example is Dwight (popularly known as: D.L.) Moody. He came from a poor home life in Northfield, Massachusetts. His father passed away when Dwight was just a young boy, leaving his family so poor that some of the children had to work for food.

As a young man, Dwight began gathering children and teaching them, resulting in the eventual founding schools for his students. God was faithful to him: seeing him through a difficult, fatherless childhood; preserving his life during the great Chicago fire; making him into a famous evangelist; and guiding him to establish Moody Bible Institute which continues to train students in the Bible for ministry throughout the world, to this day.

These three examples have a theme: people from humble circumstances accomplished great things for the eternal Kingdom, while a powerful king was brought to nothing when he forgot God. I took these lessons to heart.

Give Your Best

We must caution ourselves and others to do our best for God, not to settle for man's recognition. God is watching, and people are watching. God deserves no less from us than our very best. We have an excellent Lord. His very Name is excellent [Psalm 8:1].

A great hymn urges us from its title to the final line: "Give of Your Best to the Master." Its author, Howard B. Grose, was an ordained minister who pastored for seven years, served as President of the University of South Dakota (1890-92), taught history at the University of Chicago (1892-96), and edited the

Missions journal for 23 years. May what he penned in 1902 motivate us to follow his imperative because this convicting message has not faded over the years:

Give of your best to the Master;

Give of the strength of your youth.
Throw your soul's fresh, glowing ardor
Into the battle for truth.
Jesus has set the example,
Dauntless was He, young and brave.
Give Him your loyal devotion;
Give Him the best that you have.

Refrain: Give of your best to the Master;
Give of the strength of your youth.
Clad in salvation's full armor,
Join in the battle for truth.

Give of your best to the Master;
Give Him first place in your heart.
Give Him first place in your service;
Consecrate every part.
Give, and to you will be given;
God His beloved Son gave.
Gratefully seeking to serve Him,
Give Him the best that you have.

Give of your best to the Master;
Naught else is worthy His love.
He gave Himself for your ransom,
Gave up His glory above.
Laid down His life without murmur,
You from sin's ruin to save.
Give Him your heart's adoration;
Give Him the best that you have.

[Public Domain]

Accept That the Ultimate Reward Comes from the Lord

People often desire and seek reward for their labors. Yet our ultimate reward comes from the Lord, not from those we come in contact with as we minister doing Kingdom work.

Yes, it is gratifying to get a pat-on-the-back that keeps us encouraged. Indeed, we are called to be an encouragement to fellow believers and workers in the Kingdom and the world around us. But this world is not our home, and our ultimate reward comes from serving the Lord. The final, fullest, ultimate recognition will come from Him alone when we see Him face to face.

Mother Teresa (see chapter 3) who served the poorest of the poor in Calcutta (Kolkata), India, as a Missionary of Charity, took on poverty to live and die in a land that was not her home country. She served the largest part of her life in India, being the hands of Jesus to those who felt little or no loving human touch.

She was interested in one thing, and that was to serve Jesus, and by doing that, to serve the poor of India. She cared not for her own health or comfort, but cared much that she love others in the name of Jesus. She was a diminutive woman, but was a giant of a leader.

Mother Teresa became a beloved figure to the world, but her fame was not important. What was important to her was that she was serving her Lord. She did not consider what she did sacrificially but reached out and touched the AIDS patient and the leper, the dying, the untouchable, the aged, considering it only her little bit that she could contribute to the care for others, in the name of Jesus.

She said, "Be faithful in small things because it is in them that your strength lies." And she was the epitome of strength as she led her group of missionaries for 47 years until her death in 1997, at the age of 87. She felt privileged to travel the world, speaking out for the marginalized and hurting of society, but she made her home serving those on the streets of Calcutta. As a Godly servant leader, her life exemplified this verse:

> *Whatever you do, work at it with all your heart, as working for the Lord, not for men, since you know that you will receive an inheritance from the Lord as a reward. It is the Lord Christ you are serving.*
>
> [Colossians 3:23-24. NIV]

I love the Biblical example of David: a God-approved, God-ordained, and God-chosen leader—although an unlikely leader in the world's eyes. David served God's purpose in his own generation by first serving as a shepherd boy to his father, Jesse.

Sheep-herding was not deemed the job of a king. In fact, it was known to be a rather lowly job that not many wanted. David served under his father's authority, and he did the job, serving faithfully while fulfilling his assigned role.

He risked his life, once needing to kill a bear in order to protect the sheep entrusted to him. Later on, he had to kill a lion. He carried only a simple, ordinary slingshot for a weapon. That simple tool of defense allowed him to fearlessly defeat the giant Goliath with God directing the stone!

David had a testimony of faithfulness in the fields before arriving at his ultimate destiny. He was learning great lessons to be used when he was to be a mighty warrior, a leader of armies and a nation.

He did not know that he was headed to the throne as king over the land. Unbeknownst to him, he was in the lineage of the coming Messiah, but was not in the traditional order of that lineage to be the name attached to the head of that line. When Israel's king was crowned, all of David's other brothers were considered for the role before David; however, he was finally brought forth and named the proper choice of God and recipient of the crown. He had proven himself faithful in the lowly, humble job of sheep-herder before he was chosen to be the king of God's chosen people.

We are called and commanded to be faithful where God places us. Whether as engineer, custodian, youth pastor, or senior pastor, be faithful in that place. We cannot be a part of this "lazy" generation!

Unfortunately, there always have been, still are, and likely will continue to be many lazy people in this world who are exploiting the system for what they can do without work. But God doesn't call us to be lazy. He calls us to a life of service . . . and that means work.

Work may not seem like doing something "big" for God's Kingdom, but the book of Proverbs is full of warnings against being lazy and not working. Any little job we can do to serve is worth doing well. Dwight L. Moody succinctly and wisely worded it this way:

> Small numbers make no difference to God. There is nothing small if God is in it.

CHAPTER 7

Build Your Team

Coming together is a beginning. Keeping together is progress. Working together is success.

– Henry Ford

In 2013, when I was in Colombo, Sri Lanka, I called on Pastor Colton. He was 83 years old and pastor of a church of 10,000 people from various backgrounds.

This man and I have many mutual friends, and I asked him out to dinner in order to glean some wisdom from him. We had good conversation. After dinner as I was preparing to leave, I turned to the old pastor and asked him to share one leadership nugget.

This old African proverb is what he quoted for us:

> *If you want to go fast, go alone. If you want to go far, go together.*

I interpreted this to mean: "If you have a God-sized vision you want to fulfill, then go with a team."

When we "go together" with fellow believers, we have formed a team, and strength lies in numbers. These are familiar words, but in God's economy it is clear our strength is not in the numbers, but in the people who make up the numbers. It is in their doing things together for the Kingdom that makes the grand difference.

I give all credit to God and the capable people I have gathered around me—both now and the many helpers I have had in the past—for much I have learned in developing and doing ministry.

Failure will happen at times but, in a team, the members learn from each other and rely on one another. God created the team concept, and brings team members together to help us and to bring about His purposes. Therefore, believe in them. Trust them.

By this, I mean that we must entrust tasks to them, and by acting in such a way it brings about a multiplication effect. It is a process of growing and developing new and future leaders who will carry on the tasks at hand or begin their own tasks for the Kingdom. Here is my "Four D" system to develop team members:

1. Deliver - get them on the team by connecting with Christ.
2. Develop - develop each person based on the calling and gifting of each one.
3. Delegate - give them opportunity to use their abilities in the church and the community; get them involved.
4. Deploy - send them out when I am confident in them, with accountability.

Paul went out with a team. He did much to develop his team but, of course, he also had troubles sometimes with team mates. That is a reality, and will have to be dealt with in Godly fashion if it happens. Titus and Timothy and others were a great help to Paul in his ministry.

The Pauline epistles Paul wrote are prime examples of alluding to the team concept. For instance, Paul speaks of "all the brethren which are with me." [Galatians 1:2] He continues to address the brethren—encouraging them, warning them to be careful to follow an unperverted Gospel, and instructing them in the Lord. Paul was their team leader.

As such, he models the mindset and actions of a good leader, assuming the responsibility to be the one who encourages, gives responsibilities, warns or adMonyshes, and teaches his "team." He counted them as brothers, and speaks openly to them in Galatians.

Paul goes on to write about other team members he appears to be mentoring in leadership: Titus and Barnabas. It is obvious that, in his leadership position, he is close enough to these two men to give them clear instruction. He has no fear in adMonyshing them in areas where he feels they are not following his instructions, which God has given him for believers to follow.

Paul uses this same pattern throughout his epistles. He clearly feels a need to let the church at Corinth know that each person is different, but he still recognizes them as important members of the body of believers in Christ [I Corinthians 12].

He obviously takes his role as leader seriously enough to say the tough things, as well as to carry out the easier aspects of leading in ministry. If the tough things must be said, there is always room for forgiveness, recognition, and reconciliation.

All can profit from the mutual input of team members in symbiotic relationship, helping one another, feeding off one another, combining strengths and overcoming weaknesses. Building on the strengths of others in combination with your own strengths makes for better results than could be hoped for individually.

Ron Edmondson—a pastor with team experience in building a business, as well as guiding churches and church plants—has identified the following seven characteristics of healthy teams:

1. *Needs very little supervision*

This involves trust from the leadership. If the leader has to micromanage every movement every team member makes, it will be difficult to get anything done. A good team member will commit to get done what he or she has been assigned. This means to assign and release—very much like my "deploy" strategy.

2. *Adds to team spirit*

This requires a person working under the leader to have a loyalty to the leader, the team, the organization, and to the job to be done.

3. *Remains flexible*

This involves a sense of all working together. One fills in where another leaves a hole. We can be expected to look at other team members and know they will cover when we can't, and we will do the same.

Synergy happens when each member on the team looks out for the other and all feel their goal is for the whole group, not just for one person. Each "job" is assumed by all, even if one can complete it. In teams under Kingdom leadership, "all together" means that each is doing his or her part to bring glory to God through the team's combined work.

4. *Recognizes results as part of the reward*

As with anything, it is hoped team members can gain an intrinsic satisfaction in doing a job well. Fair compensation is just that: fair, but it should not be the reason for belonging to a team involving ministry. Achieving the team goal is the objective.

5. *Considers the interests of the entire team*

Self-serving team members are not about the team. What is needed is humble individuals looking to achieve for the good of all—team and beyond to ministry results and goals reached.

6. *Adds intrinsic value to the team*

Rewards come from without and within, and it is with the attitude that each team member brings something to the team that no one else can. Satisfaction comes from knowing you fulfill a role only you can fill and that each other team member is doing the same.

One great team member can and does transform a team. That is multiplied by the number of team members as each's input is valued.

7. *Demonstrates loyalty in action*

Each member of the team knows the vision and contributes to fulfilling it as best he or she can. Each one is supportive of the leadership, and especially in Kingdom-style leadership, recognizes that individual is in that position because of God's leading.

Direction in the overall plan is fully understood and invested in. The team member will be committed to accomplishing, following the path set, and will do that until finished unless unforeseen issues arise where it is certain God has charted a different direction.

We can thrive when the attributes of others fill in the gaps in our own abilities and contribution to a team. Like pieces in a jigsaw puzzle, the whole makes a complete picture whereas a single jigsaw piece is often not a good representation of what the whole will be when completed.

The excellence and effectiveness that any one person can bring to a project or ministry are compounded by the contributions of teammates. When we work with others, it involves taking risks, trust, cooperation, and seeing God's hand in team formation.

Take Risks

Taking risks with people means we must believe in others. We may ask the question: "What if these people fail?" But believing in others means putting our trust in them and thus taking risks.

Working alongside others in a team situation may give someone the very confidence they need to succeed. That person may learn new skills and abilities from team members. Even if someone would fail individually, the combined talents of a team could bring about success where there normally would not be triumph.

Brought to You for a Purpose

People are put into our lives for His purpose. If we look at other team members as a gift of God, an asset to the whole, we are edifying that person and giving them value because they have a purpose in God's overall plan. It may take time and effort, but we are building up people for Kingdom purposes, not for self or team gain.

The skills learned in the team setting then can be passed on as team members mature into the ability to plant and build another team. It is the shepherding effect: watch over those under our care so they grow and are safe; allow them to grow, then release them to work and build others in their own team efforts.

We do not want on our team who will say, "Yes Sir," for everything, but people who are thoughtful, willing to listen to God, and courageous enough to ask questions so that the team can make better decisions. Thus, the whole team owns the purpose of the organization. However, if a person is always negative, and works contrary to the vision, that person might not be the right person for the team.

Believe in Others

When we believe in others and believe they are brought to us for the purpose to build God's Kingdom, the result can have a multiplication effect. Like a snowball gaining girth and power as it rolls down the hill, team work picks up other people or ideas and tasks along the way, making the effort even bigger and better.

Putting faith in others is important. Big dreams involve big jobs, and that means we are going to need help from God's people. God will put people in our path who will be a good fit to work with, but there is also the possibility that there will be those who are good people, but with whom we just cannot work well together.

However, to find the right people to be partners on the team, we will need to take risks. We may discover a "poor fit" along the way; that is the cost of believing in others.

Sometimes those difficult working relationships can be rescued, with adjustments made. If so, we become stronger than before. At other times, it will mean that we must sever the working relationship—but that is no reason to sever the friendship or fellowship as fellow believers. Instead, we can release them with our blessings.

It takes time and careful consideration to choose a team. The process requires much prayer. The Bible gives clear and solid direction:

> *And the things you have heard me say in the presence of many witnesses entrust to reliable men who will also be qualified to teach others.*
>
> [II Timothy 2:2. NIV]

Recognize Strengths and Weaknesses

Of course, not everyone is a born leader, but there are many who never get to be a leader because they are not given the chance or do not acquire the confidence and skills to lead. Developing good Kingdom-style leaders requires recognizing weaknesses along with strengths.

There is always the flip side of the coin, so to speak. If someone displays vulnerability in a certain leadership trait needed for a particular task, you can think of ways the weakness can be overcome or turned into a strength.

For example, a person who has the spiritual gift of mercy might tend to get overwhelmed with the needs of those he or she is working with. Yet if that person can recognize the weakness of getting bogged down in caring to the point of becoming over-involved in the problems or needs, the weakness can be turned around to exercise the gift of mercy in a very caring way.

We must recognize that Scripture, in Jesus' own words, tells us it is not our own strength, but God's, which makes us capable of accomplishing anything for His glory:

> *. . . My grace is sufficient for you, for My power is made perfect in weakness." Therefore I will boast all the more gladly about my weaknesses, so that Christ's power may rest on me. That is why, for Christ's sake, I delight in weaknesses . . .*
>
> [II Corinthians 12:9-10a. NIV]

While writing his hymn *A Mighty Fortress* during the early 1500s, Martin Luther recognized this Godly truth: We cannot depend upon our own strength. His lyrics focus on the strength and sovereign power of God, the ultimate source of our strength, and our hope of victory over the evil one who seeks to "undo us." Consider two stanzas from that hymn:

> Did we in our own strength confide,
> Our striving would be losing;
> Were not the right Man on our side,
> The Man of God's own choosing:
> Dost ask who that may be?
> Christ Jesus, it is He;
> Lord Sabaoth, His name,
> From age to age the same,
> And He must win the battle.
>
> And though this world with devils filled,
> Should threaten to undo do us,
> We will not fear, for God hath willed
> His Truth to triumph through us:
> The Prince of Darkness grim,
> We tremble not for him;
> His rage we can endure,
> For lo, his doom is sure,
> One little word shall fell him.
>
> [Public Domain]

Ajith Fernando ThM DD serves as Teaching Director of Youth for Christ in Sri Lanka. As such, he works with teams and stresses the importance of augmenting the team structure in areas where there are identified shortages.

Believing it is better to work with a team than trying to do a task alone, he included a section titled "Growing in a Team" in his book *Jesus Driven Ministry*. Fernando explores these benefits to ministering as a team:

- Teams help with our weaknesses.
- Teams can help guide us, especially in areas of vulnerability.

- Teams can help when we are discouraged.
- Teams add depth of community to our lives.
- Teams provide us with accountability.

The work of the ministry for the Kingdom can be difficult at times, but a team can help to minimize the effects of discouragement and attacks from the enemy. If you are doing Kingdom work, the enemy will attack.

The enemy does not want to see any Kingdom work go forward. The enemy wants to see no glory given to God, and the enemy will attack in places we are most vulnerable. Teams can help prevent a lot of the effects of the enemy by being there for one another, praying together, and keeping the work going forward when one may not be able to do so alone.

Hudson Taylor and William Burns became a team of kindred spirits. They met while doing pioneer mission work in China in 1855, following a very discouraging period for Taylor. His mission board was criticizing him, and his fiancé had just broken up with him. Scottish missionary Burns was 20 years older.

Both were filled with a passion to reach the Chinese people who had never heard the name of Jesus. They immediately recognized mutual interests. As friends, they ministered dressed in traditional Chinese clothing. For seven months they worked together, walking to visit the Chinese people, giving out Bibles and Christian books, evangelizing along the way, and spending time in ministry, prayer, and fellowship.

Burns had noted the Chinese people related to Taylor in a warmer, more accepting way when he dressed like them, so he followed suit. Taylor called Burns a "spiritual father." Taylor admired Burns because of his passion for the lost, his love of God's Word, his holy lifestyle, and his deep spiritual insight. Taylor felt his life was better for the time they spent together. The insight he gained during the time they ministered together was what later gave him the foundational tenets for the organizing of China Inland Mission.

These two men provide a stellar example of teamwork that benefitted both. Burns learned how to relate in a better way to the Chinese people, and Taylor had the advantage of one-on-one with an admired, holy-living, mature, kindred spirit. In God's providence, Burns had come into Taylor's life at exactly the time he needed Godly encouragement most. This partnering blessed both parties, and both of them later recalled that period as a mutually precious time in their lives.

Moses had a unique relationship with his father-in-law Jethro—a priest of Midian. Jethro took care of Moses' wife and sons while Moses was in the wilderness. During a visit to Moses, Jethro was very interested in his son-in-law's welfare. They talked about God's work and protection in Moses' life—how the Lord had been with Moses and had saved him midst the many hardships he had endured:

> *Jethro was delighted to hear about all the good things the LORD had done from the hand of the Egyptians. He said, "Praise be to the LORD, who rescued you from the hand of the Egyptians and of Pharaoh, and who rescued the people from the hand of the Egyptians. Now I know that the LORD is greater than all other gods, for He did this to those who had treated Israel arrogantly." Then Jethro, Moses' father-in-law, brought a burnt offering and other sacrifices to God, and Aaron came with all the elders of Israel to eat a meal with Moses' father-in-law in the presence of God.*
>
> [Exodus 18:9-12. NIV]

This was clearly a visit of encouragement to Moses. Not only did he get to see his wife, Zipporah, and his two sons, but he was reminded of God's faithfulness to him because of the words of Jethro.

Moses had been in the wilderness—literally and figuratively. He had defied Pharaoh and God had led him through with victory, but he was still alone in the wilderness.

Jethro had taken care of Moses' family and his own family, but did not leave his actions at that. He also went and visited, brought family, encouraged, made a praise sacrifice, and ate a meal together. It is clearly a visit to edify a discouraged man. The greeting when they saw one another was one of affection.

Moses honored Jethro, and Jethro praised God for Moses' successes when Moses probably wasn't feeling so successful. Moses asks Jethro questions on leadership: how to deal with the people's disputes while imparting the Word of God. Jethro is concerned for Moses' welfare, telling him he is going to burn out, that this was too much for him:

> *When his father-in-law saw all that Moses was doing for the people, he said, "What is this you are doing for the people? Why do you alone sit as judge, while all these people stand around you from morning till evening?"*
>
> *Moses answered him, "Because the people come to me to seek God's will. Whenever they have a dispute, it is brought to me, and I decide between the parties and inform them of God's decrees and instructions."*
>
> *Moses' father-in-law replied, "What you are doing is not good. You and these people who come to you will only wear yourselves out. The work is too heavy for you; you cannot handle it alone. Listen now to me and I will give you some advice, and may God be with you. You must be the people's representative before God and bring their disputes to Him. Teach them His decrees and*

instructions, and show them the way they are to live and how they are to behave. But select capable men from all the people—men who fear God, trustworthy men who hate dishonest gain—and appoint them as officials over thousands, hundreds, fifties and tens. Have them serve as judges for the people at all times, but have them bring every difficult case to you; the simple cases they can decide for themselves. That will make your load lighter, because they will share it with you. If you do this and God so commands, you will be able to stand the strain, and all these people will go home satisfied."

[Exodus 18:14-23. NIV]

Moses put his father-in-law's advice into practice, and Jethro was able to go home, satisfied that his son-in-law had his burden lifted. It is not clear from Scripture whether Moses had sent messages back to Jethro or Zipporah about his discouragement, or whether Jethro went because of God's compulsion upon him to do so. Either way, there was obviously a special relationship between these two men. We should learn from the younger man's example of listening and faithfully carrying out what the older priest advised.

The counsel of mature Christians is often a wise move. We will see that pattern often brings about solutions to problems or situations we cannot navigate. The teaming up with someone like that is a worthy move. We each need that kind of person in our life. Jesus needed that in His life. He called his team of disciples "friends" in John 15:15, and recognizes that the disciples were ones with whom He could share what His Father had been sharing with Him.

Recognize and Reward

While recognition should never be the motivation for ministry, it encourages and confirms both work and calling.

Rewards, too, are not necessary, but they do edify and make one feel appreciated. Everyone needs to be appreciated at times. It certainly makes difficulties more bearable, and the good times joyful. I recognize I am not perfect, and that I have missed opportunities to recognize others at times, but I believe recognition is very, very important.

Not surprisingly, Scripture stresses a good lesson: as we submit, we make leaders jobs a joy, not a burden. One passage specifically deals with confidence in leadership.

> *Have confidence in your leaders and submit to their authority, because they keep watch over you as those who must give an account. Do this so that their work will be a joy, not a burden, for that would be of no benefit to you.*
> [Hebrews 13:17. NIV]

Divine Appointments

Throughout history, God has brought specific people together at the precise time when they need each other. Sometimes a person will team up with us for a very specific time in our life when we need it most.

As I have already noted, for Hudson Taylor and William Burns it was for a period of seven months. Correspondence may have occurred after that—although in the early 1800s, that would have been difficult. But otherwise, it is not recorded that they ever saw each other again during their lifetimes.

In the case of Moses and Jethro, it appears the wise and Godly father-in-law's visit to Moses came at God-ordained time when the younger man was weighed down by the perceived responsibilities of his leadership. Their visit resulted in advice that gave Moses much needed relief.

Many of us can look back in retrospect and see how God placed a certain person or group of people into a situation that might have been unbearable alone. Teams, whether large or small, can certainly give us the support and guidance that is needed. This is not a new concept:

> *Two are better than one; because they have a good reward for their labor. For if they fall, the one will lift up his fellow; but woe to him that is alone when he falleth; for he hath not another to help him up.*
>
> [Ecclesiastes 4:9-10. KJV]

Solomon understood the importance of teamwork. Team members lift one another up.

In Acts 2:14 we read where Peter stood up with the "other eleven." He was with a team.

In Acts 6:1-7, the disciples were so overworked with things outside of their regular duties that they felt ministry was suffering.

What did Peter and his team do? What would you do?

They expanded the team with seven others who could shoulder the burden and help lighten the load. Delegation of duties freed them for other aspects of ministry. It can do the same for team leaders today.

The selection of team members was taken seriously then, and should be today for those leading any type of team, but especially ministry teams. Godly characteristics were on the New Testament–times job descriptions and should be on ours today:

> *Brothers and sisters, choose seven men from among you who are known to be full of the Spirit and wisdom. We will turn this responsibility over to them and will give our attention to prayer and the ministry of the word.*
>
> [Acts 6:3-4. NIV]

Honest reputation . . . full of the Holy Spirit . . . wise: These are traits anyone would like to find on their team!

Jesus taught by example how teams work.

Yes, He was the One who could heal the sick, made the lame walk, caused the blind to see, and calmed a storm with the words "Peace, be still."

Yes, He cast out evil spirits, raised the dead, and forgave sins. The list could go on and on. There was nothing beyond His ability. He was God.

Yet, Jesus spent most of His time traveling with His disciples—investing time with them, leading them, teaching them, providing for them. Jesus called his team "friends" and treated them, accordingly.

> *I no longer call you servants, because a servant does not know his master's business. Instead, I have called you friends, for everything that I learned from My Father I have made known to you.*
>
> [John 15:15. NIV]

Jesus obviously counted on his friends—his team. He cared for them, related to them, and shared all God the Father had shared with Him. He didn't "need" a team. He chose to work with a team, and He didn't pick the religious leaders of the day. Instead, He picked a band of guys from varied backgrounds, and He loved them.

In calling his disciples "friends," Jesus assured them of His love for them. Knowing He was soon going to leave them in the physical sense, He instructed His team of disciples to love God and each other as He loved them.

> *My command is this: Love each other as I have loved you. Greater love has no one than this: to lay down one's*

life for one's friends. You are my friends if you do what I command.

[John 15:12-14. NIV]

Yes, Jesus knew Peter had a hot, impetuous head.

He certainly knew Luke was a respected doctor.

Sometimes, some of the team smelled of fish.

Sometimes, team members slept when they should have been alert.

Yes, Jesus knew Judas would betray Him.

Yet, even knowing everything about them, Jesus—as their friend and team leader— shared a close, personal bond with twelve specially selected men.

I try to follow Jesus' example. Over the years, I have gathered team members to work with me. I have picked people from various backgrounds for my team and invested in them to build that team concept. Today the ministry in India has grown all over the country and beyond because ordinary people became wonderful tools in the hand of God.

What a privilege to have worked along with my team members, to have helped them, as they have helped me! I am humbled to have been able to invest in their lives, as they have in mine. While I believe in promoting and recognizing team members, I admit to failures on my part to consistently model this over the years. But I keep trying, even as I know and admit my imperfections have resulted in missed opportunities. Even so, I strive to enable team members and entrust work to them, and then see they are trained and recognized for their work.

The website Bible.org offers a series on the characteristics of Christian leadership. The author—the late J. Hampton Keathley III—used the analogy of sports or business teams, which are things we hear a lot about today.

In his 17-chapter series, *Marks of Maturity: Biblical Characteristics of a Christian Leader*, Keathley expands upon the team concept:

> In the realm of sports today and even in the corporate world, we often hear the terms, *team player, team effort*. In football, the truly great running backs are usually quick to give credit to the effort of the whole team, especially the linemen, because they wisely realize a running back's ability to make yardage is dependent upon the efforts of the rest of the team.
>
> We often hear players and coaches praising members of the team as a team player. It's a quality highly regarded because it is so valuable to the team effort.
>
> It is teamwork that enables common men to do uncommon things.
>
> No organization can depend on genius; the supply is always scarce and unreliable. It is the test of an organization to make ordinary human beings perform better than they seem capable of, to bring out whatever strength there is in its members, and to use each man's strengths to help all the others perform.
>
> The purpose of an organization is to enable common men to do uncommon things.
>
> [From: Chapter titled, Mark #15: A Team Player]

And above all else, with God in the mix of a team, uncommon things will be the norm. Great things will be accomplished for His Kingdom.

CHAPTER 8

Risk Your Life for Others

"So I will very gladly spend for you everything I have and expend myself as well. If I love you more, will you love me less?"

[2 Corinthians 12:15]

Do you have a passion for developing others? Do you see developing others as a privilege? If so, you will intentionally develop opportunities for others to develop their skills and let them be in the forefront.

We risk our reputations as we put others into leadership roles and try their skills. Kingdom leadership qualities can ignite many feelings: jealousy, anger, disgust, wonder, admiration, desire for power, fear, and many others—good and bad. Risking our lives, putting our reputations on the line, giving up fame, controlling our feelings, seeing that others are being developed, and sharing in the sufferings as well as the glories of following Christ—all are ways we as Godly leaders develop credibility with those who are watching.

There is not one person who is unimportant to God [I Corinthians 12]. Dare to take risks for the ones sometimes viewed as unimportant to the world, even knowing it is not a popular stance in a world that is all about stepping on others to get ahead.

I often take a ladder into the room when I teach on servant-style leadership. It is a riveting visual to emphasize the climbing done in leading. I climb up on the ladder. If I want to demonstrate having another lead or "get ahead," I have someone else go on a higher rung or stand on my shoulders.

Some will comprehend this, while others don't like the idea of stepping on me! Shoulders can be crushed; or at least hurt. But, as I tell those in the audience, "May our lives be a ladder for others to climb higher."

In the "real world" where the ladder is metaphorical rather than a visual aid, this is not a popular stance to take. Some will be angered. In India, some will even file a case against me or will complain or report falsities to Hindu radicals and try to get me into trouble with authorities.

If someone has to be fired, that person will act in anger and try to damage the person in charge. This is what people have done in India, but that the same thing, maybe on a different scale, happens in America as well.

It will happen, but if we truly want to see others develop the skills God has given them, we must willingly take selfless risks. Jesus warned of what we should expect:

> *Very truly I tell you, unless a kernel of wheat falls to the ground and dies, it remains only a single seed. But if it dies, it produces many seeds.*
>
> [John 12:24. NIV]

A Kingdom-style leader will risk to the point of death to see others advance in the Kingdom. It's a principle we can learn. Jesus did it. The leader who is willing to risk himself or herself to further God's Kingdom rather than self-promotion is a leader who may well invite controversy and enmity. The point is clear: Leadership is risky, and risks must be taken if a leader is to be effective in the Kingdom.

"Give me India, or I die"—my edit to John Knox's famous quote, "Give me Scotland, or I die"—were the words imposed above a map of India during my days at Trinity International

University in Deerfield, Illinois, on the bedroom wall in Mony's and my apartment.

I prayed over that map, seeking God's intervention in every state of India. I had a God-given passion for India. How I would appease that passionate longing to do something for India was as yet being formed in my heart as God was leading me into a ministry to minister to my fellow Indians.

The passion I had not only did not die, it didn't even cool. God only fueled it more as I continued to seek Him on how I could assuage this passion by actually doing something constructive for my people in my homeland. I was being led to be the leader who I had been tailored to be since birth. God had been working all along.

I was not being "let off the hook." Instead, the hook sunk deeper into my willing, seeking heart. I wanted India for God, and God was preparing me to be a part of His eternal plan to reach all peoples everywhere. I was going to get my chance to see Indians come to Christ because of my involvement in God's work there.

As I developed leadership skills, I was being turned into a true Kingdom leader far different from what leaders usually are in the world's eyes. True Kingdom leaders risk much to see others thrive.

I wanted my staff, the national missionaries, and the unsaved to thrive—to live a life of abundance in Christ. True Kingdom leaders have a passion to bring out the potential in others.

Early on, it became evident I was a born teacher and leader. As such, I could develop people and ministries which would develop the next generation of leaders and bring others to places where they could know and serve Jesus as Lord.

True Kingdom leaders take chances on others who have not yet been able to prove themselves, often intentionally creating opportunities for developing hidden potential. I was evangelizing and discipling others long before I helped birth the RIMI and MI ministries. I was putting people into places of leadership and service where they could learn their calling on their lives.

True Kingdom leaders desire to see others grow and mature into leaders. I had been developing siblings, friends, and acquaintances to work in ministry where they could recognize their own abilities.

True Kingdom leaders are not threatened by the success of others, and they will risk their own reputation to give others a chance to succeed. I was never threatened that others might get ahead of me in ministry. In fact, I welcomed putting people in place where they would shine and gain skills of their own.

I would risk my own dignity and life to see others noticed and credited, not needing notice or credit myself. Risking all to further the Kingdom is to look for other potential workers and leaders who:

- have a passion for developing others;
- intentionally create opportunities for others;
- will risk their own reputations;
- are ready to be betrayed and denied;
- view servanthood as key, and put self last.

In Mark 10:35-45 we have the story of James and John as two brothers trying to get ahead. They used their positions as Jesus' friends to insure they were closer to Him than anyone else. James and John were not exactly the picture of leaders captivated by putting others ahead. They were expecting Jesus to do whatever they asked—not asking Jesus what He wanted them to do. This seems to be a bit of a backward approach when they knew the Son of God so well!

They knew His servant leadership style. They had been told He was God's own Son. So why were they, of all the disciples, expecting or seeking to be closest to Jesus? It's easy for us to see, from our two-thousand-years-later perspective, they were both thinking of the principle of self first, not last. And they were familiar with Him, not intimate as yet with His heart.

Jesus' reply is so wonderful. In today's language He asks, "Boys, what is you want Me to do for you?"

James and John told Jesus they wanted to be the ones sitting on His right and left sides in His glory; His Kingdom. We can assume they were thinking about thrones when they referred to "Thy glory" [KJV]. They were thinking that they were worthy to receive basically the same accolades as God Himself.

In contemporary terms, what Jesus warms them is essentially: "Boys, you don't know what you're asking." He then asks them if they are willing to go through the suffering and death with Him as He was soon going to have to do.

They obviously did not understand what was ahead. They assured Jesus they could. But not one could go through what Jesus was to go through to pay the price for all of the sins of the world, past and present.

Besides, they were not the ones to go through what was ahead as ordained by God's perfect plan—only the perfect Son of God could fulfill the plan put into place before time began. Jesus assured them they would go through what He was going to go through, but not yet.

This was later brought about when both were martyred because of this Man they were following. But first Jesus had to pay the price for them as well.

When the other disciples heard what the sons of Zebedee had asked, they were "indignant" [NIV]. Jesus then gives His timeless lesson on what a Kingdom leader has to be. He tells them three things:

1. Those regarded as rulers by the world are going "to lord it over" those they rule

2. Those who are rulers, have higher rulers over others who do the very same thing

   This concept is so true in India. Without bribes, it is almost impossible to do anything. Even to get a job, one must pay money. The weak of this world are having authority exercised over them. This is what is happening all over the world. In Jesus' Kingdom values are different. Jesus told His disciples it will not be the same for them. They are to have different values, not crave greatness.

3. Anyone who wants to be great in the Kingdom of God, has to be a servant. Jesus' message [echoed in Matthew 20:26] was if we want to do great things—which is what God calls us all to do through and for Him—we must be servants in our minds and hearts, attitudes and actions.

   Servants of that day would have had little freedom, but a slave would have had absolutely no freedom. Only a master could decide what a slave could or could not do. The slave had no choice. Jesus continues: to be first in His Kingdom. As His servants, even if we are given a chance to go first, we are to let another go first.

To put it colloquially, "Don't be in a hurry to get on the bus." We can still get on the bus, but shouldn't push and shove to be first in line. We will still be on the bus if we are the last one on and get the last seat, or even have to stand. The difference is, if we have stepped aside to let others get on before us, then we are doing what Jesus was talking about. To be last exemplifies the Kingdom perspective: letting others be first, acted out for the sake of Jesus and His expectation of a real leader.

Jesus concludes this Mark 10 passage with an example from His own life experience:

For even the Son of Man did not come to be served, but to serve, and to give His life as a ransom for many.

[Mark 10:45. NIV]

Jesus talked about His problems, and what He expected from His people. What He told them was something they did not expect to hear. He certainly wasn't assigning seats of preference and high position! No, He was telling them to be servants and slaves. This was radical!

However, they did fulfill what Jesus told them that day. They later, after Jesus' resurrection and ascension, did partake of the same "cup" He took. As for the sons of Zebedee, tradition tells us that James was beheaded in Jerusalem, and John was first boiled in oil and, when that failed to kill him, was exiled to the prison island of Patmos. John was the only one of those to whom Jesus spoke that day who died of old age, but even that was not without persecution. The disciples finally "got it." Jesus' words helped them be faithful (except for Judas, the betrayer) to Him to their earthly end. We must do the same: risk our lives for the sake of others to develop leaders.

Another example is Barnabas risking his life in Acts 9:26-30. Paul had just escaped death threats by going over the Jerusalem city wall in a basket, and the first place he headed was to join other believers. However, they were fearful of Paul because of his past life as persecutor of Christians; Paul's reputation was bad.

Barnabas put his life and reputation on the line by telling how Paul's dramatic encounter on the road to Damascus resulted in his being a changed man.

> *. . . Barnabas took him and brought him to the apostles. He told them how Saul [Paul] on his journey had seen the Lord and that the Lord had spoken to him, and how in Damascus he had preached fearlessly in the name of Jesus.*
>
> [Acts 9:27. NIV]

Only after Barnabas' intervention was Paul accepted and able to begin his preaching life only to be under threat of his life again with some Grecian Jews he had debated. His Christian brothers then sent Paul back to Tarsus, his home area.

After that, Paul traipsed from place to place often with death threats over his head as he became the apostle, leader, and writer of epistles, eventually ending up imprisoned in Rome where he finally was martyred for his faith in the Jesus he had once so adamantly opposed.

At times, risking does involve hurt and frustration. A person in ministry must be willing to take the risks in order to develop people for the Kingdom.

The 1800s' American theologian William GT Shedd said, "A ship is safe in harbor, but that is not what a ship was built for."

In keeping with principles of Kingdom-style leadership, we could paraphrase that by saying, "A leader is safe in the office, but that is not what God developed a leader for."

CHAPTER 9

Ask Courageously

Ask and it will be given to you; seek and you will find; knock and the door will be opened to you

[Matthew 7:7]

When God's Kingdom work needs resources, I ask! Whether those needs are money, materials, physical labor, or spiritual support as in counseling or prayer, or emotional support through needy situations, etc. etc., I ask!

My first plan of action, after much prayer, is to ask others to help meet the need, whatever it might be.

Consider who the need is for. Needs must be made known in order for resources to be supplied. Needs are not met unless provisions are made.

Granted, it is humbling to have to ask others for help, but we must ask. Although it does take humility, at times, more often it takes blatant courage.

Be bold: Jesus tells us to ask!

> *You do not have because you do not ask God. 3 When you ask, you do not receive, because you ask with wrong motives, that you may spend what you get on your pleasures*
>
> (James 4:2b-3, NIV)

Next, let's consider nine Biblically-based principles of the leadership quality of being courageous enough to ask:

1. Share your need.
2. Specify your need.
3. Give a compelling reason.
4. Be unafraid to ask.
5. Ask the right person.
6. Asking of God.
7. Asking for life change.
8. Anticipate rejection, but rejoice.
9. Express profound gratitude.

Share Your Need

A wise friend once said something like this: "If you don't tell us your needs, we don't know about them, and we then cannot go with you vicariously on this journey. Maybe I will never be able to go on an actual physical mission, but if I help you go, then I get to go vicariously."

In other words, if needs aren't made known, we actually rob others of the opportunity to be involved in mission when they cannot go along physically.

Senders are essential in order for there to be *goers*.

Goers have no one to go to unless there are receivers. At each step of this sending-going-receiving process, the possibility arises only because needs have been identified, made known in a compelling way, and then met by those God has enabled to do so.

Specify Your Need

Another wise friend once told me, "Be specific!"

What good advice for praying—as well as the requests made known to potential donors and supporters. Those people want to invest in Kingdom work in some capacity. Let them know specifically how they can be useful.

People tend to be moved to give so much more when they hear of specific needs rather than general requests. While generalities only speak to a few, more people tend to get excited about details: people with real names and faces, and projects that speak to hearts.

This is also a way to encourage others to become involved over a longer period of time, rather than just a one-time gift of money or service. When we invest in a particular project, our human nature makes us want to see it through to completion, as our interests are often in the finished or final outcome.

By the time a particular need is met and a project is finished, we have become invested in prayer and giving, and may have formed a bond.

Trouble may arise if prayer and caring are not invested; and when the project is finished, involvement also comes to an end. Sometimes that works, as God calls some to specific involvement only.

If the need is specified as part of a whole, and people are invested, especially through prayer, they can become involved in an on-going, ministry-wide need that involves partnering over the long haul.

That is why prayer is vital to ministry. Prayer and giving should go hand in hand. Then, as we identify and present specific needs, God helps respondents see how their contributions—whether in prayer, giving, or service of some kind—can fit into the ministry as a whole.

Give a Compelling Reason

It is much more compelling to give when the reason for the need to give is made known to the giver, rather than when he is asked as a general request. Asking must be genuinely compelling. Articulating the reason is central to success.

Being specific is good only to the point that it becomes uninteresting. Give details, yes—but not to the point of providing so many that the purpose and reasons are lost. Also, people like to hear why the need exists and specifically how they can become a part of meeting it.

In the work MI and RIMI do through the Mercy Homes, much of the success of the program is because individuals get photos of children in dire need. A needy child is a God-given compulsion to tenderhearted people who actually see the photo of a real person who needs food, clothing, housing, livelihood, education, and a chance to learn about Jesus. The request to give is made known in juxtaposition to the need. Accompanied with the photo, it can be the means God lays the request urgently on the hearts of people to become involved in supporting this ministry of mercy.

Be Unafraid to Ask

I am always unafraid to ask for help for the work in India. Why? Because I know that the resources, money and any possessions or gifts given and received are ultimately God's resource, money, and possessions anyway. He has entrusted what He owns to people and also gives the "temporary holders" the desire to give up those resources to benefit the Kingdom.

God has placed those resources in the hands of people for a purpose: to provide for their own needs, and to give back to God. That allows people to become involved in ministry in different capacities according to their resources.

Another reason I am not afraid to ask is because it is never for my personal needs, but always for the poor and marginalized people who exist without a chance to know God unless someone goes and gives and tells them the Gospel story.

With the Gospel at the center of all RIMI does, why should

I or anyone on our ministry be afraid to ask God's people for resources? The same should be true for any God-driven, God-honoring ministry.

The actual asking often releases people and empowers them to be able to be involved in ministry. When someone asks others to give, it opens the doorway to opportunity for those who want to share the blessings God has bestowed on them.

An illustrative story of this truth came out when Peter Jennings, the late charismatic ABC news anchor, went to Calcutta to report on Mother Teresa's death and funeral. In Jennings' typically engaging fashion, he reported on how passionate Mother Teresa was about her work.

I will never forget watching this particular newscast with interest; seeing and hearing Jennings report from Calcutta. He told about Mother Teresa going to the house of the governor of the state of California. She went, with the sole intent of asking for a building in downtown Los Angeles to house the Missionaries of Charity order she headed worldwide.

The governor was out, so Mother Teresa went directly to the governor's wife, insisting that she see the governor. The governor's wife called her husband, telling him Mother Teresa was at their house. This brought him home quickly!

The governor asked Mother Teresa what she needed, and her reply was direct. She knew about a particular unused building in downtown Los Angeles that she needed for her work.

She asked. And the governor of California made sure she got it!

Almost, comically, Mother Teresa probably didn't even

realize her worldwide impact would cause governors to rush to her side! In her humble fashion, all she was thinking about was the need for housing the mission work her Missionaries of Charities did throughout Los Angeles.

Yes, she was a tiny woman, but she served a powerful God and found her boldness in her relationship with Him. In this instance, she got a building because she was not afraid to ask.

Have you ever wondered who funded the costs for stadiums and other expenses for big projects, like the Billy Graham Crusades? As noted before, although Billy Graham came from humble beginnings, God allowed him to evangelize millions all over the world. How was this possible?

The reason is that Billy Graham was not afraid to ask businessmen to finance the crusades. Others freely giving of their resources enabled Billy Graham to preach freely to large crowds—and many responded to the message to follow Christ.

To accomplish great things, we must be willing to ask. At one time, I was fearful to ask for any help. When I began attending TEDS and had spent most of my money on an old Oldsmobile that I needed for transportation, I wondered how I would be able to live in the Chicago area.

Sometimes I went to my post office box at seminary, and there I would find an envelope containing the money I needed to survive. To this day, I do not know who put money there. All I know is that God was providing for me through someone else's obedience to God's nudging that they were to give; to invest in Kingdom work they believed I would do.

Based on those experiences, God provided the boldness I needed to enable me to ask for bigger ministry needs, partly because God had been so faithful to provide in times of my own financial crises.

Ask the Right Person

God puts people together at specific times to complete His work. My personal philosophy is to ask the right person. One must develop the ability to be willing to delve into others' abilities and to understand people. If people's preferences are known, those preferences may be the avenue which matches them to a specific need in the mission.

Prayer is vital to this process of matching interests to the right people. God can open the minds of people to give, as well as the mind of the seeker of gifts, to ask the exact right person who is willing to give to a particular need that appeals to him or her.

Once, when I had returned from a trip to India, I was speaking at the church I attended in Wheeling. I shared what God was doing, and gave projections of what I believed in my heart God would do in the future. At that time, I was driving a school bus for income. The job took a large chunk of time out of each day, and left me with too little time to do the ministry work in RIMI that I increasingly felt called to do.

Simultaneously, my family back in India was counting heavily on me sending money back monthly to help them live, so I felt compelled to continue earning money through the bus-driving job. Then once, while speaking at church, I felt a leading from God that I should approach every member of the Wheeling Evangelical Free Church and ask them to help. To forestall future misunderstandings, I first consulted with the pastor.

I am sure he must have been worried about my radical plan, but he heard me out. That church had watched me for the four years I had been in seminary, and I believed they would be willing and ready to act on the groundwork I had been laying for those years.

The result was they, the RIMI board which had been set up by that time, helped me buy the small building that housed the beginning of RIMI. The church partnered with me and helped establish the RIMI ministry that God had called me to start. Early on I was fearful but, knowing the need for this in India, continued to go ahead with what I felt compelled to begin to do, as the Holy Spirit led.

Asking for God

Anytime I ask for donations for the work that RIMI does in India, I know it is for God's work there. Gifts represent investment in people. The work is all about the Gospel . . . all about making the fame of His Name known to the people groups throughout India . . . all about introducing people to Jesus, people who have never heard the Name of Jesus before.

If the glory of Christ is made known, then people who recognize that glory will respond to the God of glory. That is the reason asking is a joy, not a burden. It is all for Him. All of it is about Him. It is to exalt Him and make Him known.

As noted before, Corrie ten Boom—the well-known Auschwitz survivor, public speaker, and author—viewed ownership of things of this world with exactly the right attitude when she echoed Martin Luther in saying:

> I have held many things in my hands, and I have lost them all; but whatever I have placed in God's hands, that, I still possess.

After all, we "own" nothing but that which God has provided us. Everything we see, use, enjoy, or desire is His. God has a way of putting into our hands more than we can think to ask for. When we treat those gifts with eternity's values in mind, He rewards us in eternal benefits.

We may hold things in our hands for a while—literally, or figuratively—but when we realize nothing is ours, it becomes easier to relinquish it, to return it to the Giver of all things. We "own" only what God has allowed, and His Word clearly tells us what Corrie ten Boom had learned and proclaimed:

> *For every beast of the forest is Mine, and the cattle upon a thousand hills.*
>
> [Psalm 50:10. KJV]

Since the Creator God owns it all, we really only ask that His resources be given by us to further the Kingdom work we are doing. This is the long and short of asking: It is for God. Asking or giving, one or the other or both, is how our part of being involved in His Kingdom work plays out.

If we don't ask, we don't receive. John 16:24 tells us to ask so that "your joy may be full." Asking makes us joyful, but there is a higher reason: We ask to further His glory, not for ourselves or for our fame—only His.

The flip side of the coin is when we humble ourselves to do the asking for Him, we are privileged to participate in the process as He has chosen to work in and through people. The need ultimately represents people helping people. The money and resources are not what it is about; it is about people.

The gifts given are a means to an end, and that is the bottom line: It affects people. When we ask others to give of their resources and selves for God's work, the purpose is help bring people into the Kingdom.

Asking for Life Change

The motivation behind making appeals for donations is ultimately to make God's glory known to the nations. That means when we ask people to give to the ministry, the people on the receiving end in India then have the resources to go forth to make His glory known in a place you cannot be.

By asking others to give, we allow them to help make His glory known, and they are part of the ministry, albeit from a distance. Maybe a person's gift can release a national pastor from the time it would take to work for food and necessities for his family. How exciting to be part of making this happen—of giving, even if not always knowing the specific need but trusting the Holy Spirit's leading. If the necessities are provided, and the pastor is free to spend time evangelizing and church planting in addition to having more time with his family, no gift is given in vain.

When God's glory is revealed and people acknowledge His glory, lives change. God's people enjoy hearing of lives transformed, especially when they hear about something in which they had a part. We are to enjoy our journey in life when we know Christ. Giving can be a part of that joy. And rejoicing in hearing of the results of souls for His Kingdom follows.

Our life changes as we give, as it will for the recipients when they are able to utilize our gifts to change their own lives and the lives of those they minister to in Jesus' name.

Expect Rejection, But Rejoice

Of course, when people are asked to give, some will reject the opportunity. There will be those who respond negatively, but that is not cause for discouragement. In everything we are to give thanks. Scripture instructs us to rejoice all the time. Our joyful thanks should not be contingent on happy or gratifying circumstances, but on Who God is.

> *Rejoice in the Lord always. I will say it again: Rejoice! Let your gentleness be evident to all. The Lord*

is near. Do not be anxious about anything, but in every situation, by prayer and petition, with thanksgiving, present your requests to God.

[Philippians 4:4-6. NIV]

Rejoice always, pray continually, give thanks in all circumstances; for this is God's will for you in Christ Jesus.

[I Thessalonians 5:16-18. NIV]

There are lessons God wants to teach us in both the times we're on the receiving end and the times when we feel rejection. Job tells us that God gives and takes away, and we are to bless Him anyway. That includes even when our requests are met with God's "No," or His silence, or His "Not yet, not now."

Rejoicing is a gift that only God through His Holy Spirit can provide: to give thanks and have joy even in times that we do not get what we want or ask for. You are always a recipient of the best that God wants for you! Whenever I am given the opportunity, I share the need of my ministries. The outcome is up to God.

Express Profound Gratitude

Both of the Scriptural passages above refer to joy, thankfulness, along with the idea of "always" or "all the time"—with prayer. The King James Version of the Philippians passage phrases it "but in everything by prayer and supplication, with thanksgiving, let your requests be made known to God." Similarly, in the Thessalonians section, we are instructed: "in everything give thanks."

Thanksgiving to both God and the people involved in His work is not really an option, according to the Apostle Paul, but involves gratefulness in every circumstance: therefore we must

- Thank people for providing needs.
- Thank people for the opportunity to share needs with them even if they do not want to be involved or are unable to at a specific time.
- Thank people for their part in God's work.
- Thank God for the opportunity to be involved in Kingdom business.

Gratefulness to be able to partner with givers, receivers, and our Maker is all part of a package that should be bathed in gratitude for every part of the opportunities God gives us to make Him known.

The pioneer missionary to India who became known as the "father of modern missions," William Carey (1761–1834) once heard this remark at a missions-focused meeting: "There is a gold mine in India, but it seems almost as deep as the center of the earth. Who will venture to explore it?"

Carey's response was, "I will venture to go down, but remember that you must hold the ropes." He was saying that, even though he was the one making the actual journey to India to live and spend his life there, he could not do it unless he had the support of the mission society and people who sent him.

For over 40 years Carey labored in India, never returning to his homeland. But he was well aware he needed physical and spiritual support in prayer and resources to undertake the work he did. This included translation, education in various capacities, business, reforms for marginalized people, and the support of other missionaries in India.

Carey was able to do what he did—amid hardships, family problems, sorrow, and many difficulties—because there were fellow laborers in India, spouses, family, and those back in England that helped to "hold his ropes." This whole idea of giving people the opportunity to be involved in mission was also addressed by Henri Nouwen. He packed a lot of ministry into a relatively short life (1932-1996) as Dutch priest, professor, writer, and theologian, as espoused this radical (at least, by worldly standards) philosophy:

> Asking people for money is giving them the opportunity to put their resources at the disposal of the Kingdom.

This viewpoint promotes giving as a legitimate way to be involved in Kingdom work. How will others know needs unless they are informed, and how will they be involved unless they are given the opportunity? If we who are passionately involved in ministry desire to accomplish great things, we must ask other to join us because God does His work through people He draws to Himself, and whom He guides and gifts for gifting.

CHAPTER 10
Kingdom Perspective

Jesus, unlike the founder of any other major faith,
holds out hope for ordinary human life.
Our future is not an ethereal, impersonal form
of consciousness. We will not float through the air,
but rather will eat, embrace, sing, laugh, and dance
in the kingdom of God, in degrees of power, glory,
and joy that we can't at the present imagine."

– Timothy Keller

The Kingdom of God is mentioned multiple times in the New Testament and was central to Jesus' message to the world. God calls us to join in His mission to build His Kingdom, which Jesus came to establish. The Kingdom is within believers who are called and privileged to join God in His mission.

But what is this thing called Kingdom? It is God's rule and reign in a place to reflect His glory. Each of us can be a reflection, or evidence, of the Kingdom—but only with His help. One anonymous source said,

> The Kingdom of God is where God is and where God lives with His people for fulfilling His mission of redeeming all of His creation to Himself.

It is not about you, or me, or even a collective "us." It is always thinking God's Kingdom first. This is contrary to human nature which constitutes a misshapen sense of self, so it takes much prayer and yielding to God to be able to have that Kingdom perspective.

Human nature makes us so prone to wanting to promote ourselves; in and of ourselves, we beg for recognition. That is why we must rely on the Spirit within us to take the desires for our own gratification away and replace it with wanting to throw our sense of self into God's Kingdom purposes, for His glory and our fulfillment.

It is this Kingdom perspective that helps us to work effectively with people from different backgrounds and cultures. If we are serving God, and someone from the other side of the globe is following God, we have an immediate affinity that only God can give because of the love we both have for Him. It amounts to instant common ground and camaraderie.

The most important relationship in my life is the same as my fellow laborer. Our loyalties are united in Christ. Although the reasons are similar in each region, these are advantages or benefits of living and working with this Kingdom perspective in mind.

It Is a Privilege

We have a Divine invitation to work in and on what God wants: building His Kingdom. We can enjoy His favor and His help as we are fulfilling His plan and purpose on earth with eternal values in mind. There is nothing more awesome than to be assured in our hearts that we labor for the sake of the Kingdom, to make God's glory known.

It is an absolute privilege to walk alongside and to be intimately involved with Him as Savior, but also as a partner in ministry. He wants to work with us. The God of the Universe loved us enough to send His only Son to pay for all each of us have done or will do wrong so that we can be in right relationship with Him.

That, my friend, is a privilege.

It Is Within You

We are not building our own kingdom, so there should be no competition. What we build is for God's glory. This may be practically difficult, but it is a blessing to others and a witness for unbelievers to see. We can bless others to do well even if they aren't in the same work as we are, as long as they, too, are doing Kingdom work.

What a freedom we all would enjoy if this was put to practical application! There have been too many ministries abandoned, diminished, or destroyed because of favoritism and jealousy. When the focus veers away from the One whose Kingdom we are ministering to build, the results are disastrous.

So when we each yield self and think in a Kingdom perspective, there is freedom in promoting others and their ministry efforts because it is all and only about the eternal Kingdom. It is within us to give up self-promotion when the focal point is God and His Kingdom.

Work in Unity

Unity with others is possible when both parties are working for Christ's Kingdom on earth. In a Kingdom situation, there is no competition between mission organizations and denominations, or people "different" from us but still Christ's followers.

People can recognize the ability to work toward the common goal of Kingdom building. Disunity is often the cause of much heartache and loneliness in ministry work. This happens when people are "doing their own thing," opposing those in similar ministries when their goals are quite comparable. Yet they exist in a vacuum, refusing to work together because the work is not seen as Kingdom work, but "our" or "my" work.

If our eyes are fixed on the cross, then others with that same focus will have their eyes pointed in the same direction. Then, working together for the sake of the Kingdom becomes a joy, not a hindrance or cause of jealousy and disunity. Sadly, too many denominations and organizations in India do not work together.

God has humbled me to see there is a greater cause than just MI. Sometimes members of other groups refuse to attend MI functions, but I still go to their functions. There is something much larger, the Kingdom of God—that we all should work together to build on this earth.

It Brings Humility

Kingdom work brings glory to God, not self. Self-promotion is so unnecessary and totally unproductive. When the work becomes all about God, human desires are immersed in His desires. Working with that perspective, no self-recognition is needed. God does the blessing as He lifts up those working for Him. This kind of effort is not proud or puffed up.

> *. . . be clothed with humility: for God resisteth the proud, and giveth grace to the humble. Humble yourselves therefore under the mighty hand of God, that He may exalt you in due time.*
>
> [I Peter 5:5b-6. KJV]

God will give the credit when it is due. That is what is important. Leave the timing to Him! This is the very best kind of acknowledgment we could receive: recognition from a holy, mighty God who offers eternal value for our efforts, and has our very best interests at heart—those purposes which do and will further His Kingdom.

Francis Chan, the author and preacher who is inarguably considered to be a Kingdom leader in evangelistic circles today, comments on humility in leadership without using the word "humble"—

> If your family, friends, and congregation have better things to say about you than God, it's because you give them that impression . . . Whenever a church leader is named more than God, it is questionable who is most important. I think there has been too much emphasis on me. I want to be used by God, but I think we have this desire to make heroes out of people rather than following God and the Holy Spirit . . . Even in my own church I heard the words, "Francis Chan" more than I heard the words, "Holy Spirit."
>
> [From the video, "*Why Authentic Leadership Matters*"]

Chan's words underscore the premise that Kingdom-style leadership cannot be about the leader or the team members. It is about God and His fame. After all, He knows everything about us and sees what we do [Revelations 3:1]. We always come up short in comparison to the glory of God Almighty [Romans 3:23].

You and I have no excuse, and we have no right to sit in judgment on anyone else [Romans 2:1-4] because in the very act of thinking we are worthy to be above others, we have pronounced judgment on ourselves. No one possesses the righteousness [Romans 3:10] needed to stand before a holy God and claim worthiness, leaving it only by God's mercy and grace that we can do anything at all.

Yet God loves us anyway, and allows us to work with and for Him. He desires a close and meaningful relationship with each of us. It is truly astonishing how He much loves us in spite of our unrighteousness.

Almighty God wants us on His team as we lead others.

It Gives Credit to Others

A humble Kingdom-style perspective allows us to give credit to anyone because it is not about us, it is about God and what He wants to establish in our hearts and in our world. We view others differently:

Do nothing out of selfish ambition or vain conceit, but in humility consider others better than yourselves.

[Philippians 2:3. NIV]

Working together, we make each other better. God unites us, so giving Him credit allows us to give credit to the people we team with; those who follow us; those we follow, as together we serve Christ.

As iron sharpens iron, so one person sharpens another.

[Proverbs 27:17 NIV]

It Is Easy to Forgive Others

On this point, allow me, as a Christian brother, to pose a penetrating question (and one I also ask myself): If someone wrongs you, can you forgive them? It's an uncomfortable question, isn't it?

We can forgive offenders, if our focus is on bringing fame to God's name, not our own. We can forgive others, if we keep short accounts. We can forgive those who have "trespassed against us," in the words of The Lord's Prayer, if and when we learn to forgive as God, through Christ, forgives us.

Forgiveness can be a very difficult obstacle for some to overcome. If an unforgiving spirit reigns in our hearts, we will have trouble and bitterness, not the release true forgiveness brings us. The reason is because the focus is on what we feel, not on Who has forgiven us.

Andy Stanley, pastor of a church in Atlanta, Georgia, elucidates this challenging truth about forgiveness:

> In the shadow of my hurt, forgiveness feels like a decision to reward my enemy. But in the shadow of the cross, forgiveness is merely a gift from one undeserving soul to another
>
> [From: *Enemies of the Heart:*]

I can honestly echo Pastor Stanley, that I am as underserving of forgiveness as anyone. Yet, Christ in mercy and grace gave me the powerful act of forgiveness personified when He died on the cross. He died to forgive me of my sins—that is the Gospel we are to share with everyone.

Every act of forgiveness we offer to another is forgiving that one for the wrong or sin done against us. In forgiving others, we follow the Divine plan set forth in Scripture and modeled by Jesus Himself throughout his ministry and on the cross.

When we harbor a lack of forgiveness within, we are really allowing a person or an incident to have a lot of power over us. If we release that person or incident to Jesus who forgave us, we also release the hold that person or happening has on our feelings and life.

> *And be ye kind one to another, tenderhearted, forgiving one another, even as God for Christ's sake hath forgiven you.*
>
> [Ephesians 4:32. KJV]

Enjoy Ministry

"Enjoy?" you ask.

"Yes!" I can assure you, based on personal experience.

Without a Kingdom perspective, we can only strive, not

thrive. There is no life-sustaining power in anger, fatigue, burnout, and or jealousy. Whatever you endeavor becomes a burden. There is no joy. Burn-out hits hard and the ultimate result is to hate what we are doing.

The enormity and difficulty of the task is just not worth it if it is about us, and we have to worry whether we are appreciated or recognized enough. God instructs us to build His Kingdom, and when He tells us to do something, He does two things:

1. He equips us to do the task.
2. His presence is with us all the way.

With those two blessings alone, the burden of self -accomplishment is alleviated. The idea of it all being about the Kingdom allows us to enjoy ministry and relax. We no longer have to worry about keeping a tight grip on the ministry, which is God's anyway.

I admit that this mindset did not come easily for me. I had a hard time when he was younger, in earlier days of this ministry. When someone left MI for other work and took things MI had given them, I and the Nagpur staff had a hard time with it.

If they took a motor bike that MI had given them, it caused hard feelings. I had to ask myself, "Who gave the motor bike?" I knew the answer: "God's people gave it for the ministry."

When I thought about it, I realized they were taking a motor bike they had been using, and would continue to use, for ministry; and I just needed to release the bike and the people to God and let them go with a blessing. The idea of it all being for God's Kingdom gave me relief and I could release my feelings of hurt or hard feelings.

Then, I could enjoy ministry more. I didn't have to worry who the property belonged to, and I was relieved to be able to relax my position and sleep well.

Doing otherwise only creates anger. Natural inclination—human nature—want to seek revenge, and God's blessing is lost. After all, God has allowed us to work in His Kingdom, so who are we to demand ownership of anything involved?

To enjoy ministry, we must ask God for a "daily humbling" and reminders that there is no ownership on our part. We can give up our "rights" and release to God what is already His.

A recent devotional reading spoke to me about enjoying my ministry:

> *Therefore, you kings, be wise; be warned, you rulers of the earth. Serve the Lord with fear and rejoice with trembling. Kiss the Son, lest He be angry and you be destroyed in your way, for His wrath can flare up in a moment. Blessed are all who take refuge in Him.*
>
> [Psalm 2 10-12. NIV]

Any position we have, any leadership entrusted to us, we are to view it with humility and fear because God in His mercy has entrusted it to us—possibly through human channels, but make no mistake: it is all from God and part of His plan. All authority comes from God.

Everything.

Yes: everything.

All our titles, positions, possessions, reputations—all came from God. Therefore, we should serve the Lord with fear. Every time when you or I stand in the pulpit and preach to the people, we must remember that all came from God. Therefore (and I say this with great passion): Serve the Lord with trembling and fear.

Banana-Tree–Style versus Banyan-Tree–Style Leadership

The analogy of being either a banana-tree–style leader or a banyan-tree–style leader can be looked at in the following ways:

The *banana* comes from a shoot of a flowering plant, not even classified as a true tree. After every harvest it dies down and produces new plants from a bulb-like structure at the bottom or root area. It is a one-season plant and produces much fruit.

The banana needs plenty of water, but other plants and banana "trees" can thrive around them because they don't take up all the nourishment or light. Bananas grow in a lot of nations of the world and produce food for many people.

A mature *banyan* tree is quite impressive. It grows big and offers much shade. Nothing grows beneath its hefty leaves and multiple trunks—only more banyan trunks. It is considered a part of the fig family, but only one type of fig tree produces an edible fruit—and it is not this one. The roots come down all over the place off the limbs, claiming more and more land.

A *banyan* tree is all about putting out more roots and shoots and trunks, and each competes for light to survive. It covers a large area and is a sort of "forest of one" as multiple trunks grow from the original host tree, often killing it making the multi-trunked marvel dead and hollow in the center.

The *banana* is all about producing fruit and reviving its "root" system into new banana plants for the coming season.

The *banyan* is all about making more of itself to the point of destroying the original, all without an edible fruit.

Do you want to produce fruit and see others rise up around you? Or do you just want to make more of yourself until you are completely spent and hollow on the inside without fruit to profit anyone but yourself?

It would be easy to expand this banana-banyan analogy further, but I hope I have presented my point clearly. Christ needs those who spend themselves for the Kingdom, not for self. He doesn't want to see his team completely spent, promoting themselves to the detriment of the core purpose.

Do you put out impressive fruit or impressive trunks? What kind of leader are you: banana-style, or banyan-style?

CHAPTER 11

Absolute Confidence in God

Faith is deliberate confidence in the character of God whose ways you may not understand at the time.
– Oswald Chambers

Even throughout all the difficulties experienced in many areas of my life, once I began to follow Christ, I was gifted with an unshakable confidence in God. When I gave my life to Him, for me it was everything, no halfway measures.

Without Christ, I realized I could do nothing. With Christ, I could do anything. All the ministry visible to those who go to India and see the Nagpur campus is not because somebody gave money. No; the money came later on. It all came about by faith in God.

The story unfolding and now evident in Nagpur exhibited the truth of this verse:

> *I can do all things through Christ which strengtheneth me.*
>
> [Philippians 4:13. KJV]

With Bible in-hand, I studied and strengthened my resolve to follow what was modeled by Biblical characters who, like me, were each on a spiritual journey, allowing God to reveal His plan for their lives in His time. I also found personal heroes within the annals of the more contemporary Christian movement. One common thread ran through Biblical and biographical (or autographical) accounts: absolute confidence in God's love and unfailing promises.

Applying what I learned from those studies encouraged me. As I faced challenges, I found no need to feel, think, or worry,

"If God doesn't answer me on this, what will I do then?" I was given the gift of complete trust in the God of the Bible and the God of today.

I was blessed! I knew I need never doubt that God would provide all my needs and do what was best for me, my family, and the ministry God chose for me and for which He was preparing me.

That does not mean that I never felt the weight of my responsibilities; it simply meant I placed it in God's powerful hands where it belonged and where it was anyway. I left it there in God's care because of my trust in God's grace and mercy. I was learning that:

> *. . . without faith it is impossible to please [God]*
> [Hebrews 11:6. NKJV]

The faith of many Biblical heroes was impacting my life as I fully relied on God with a confidence that matched my determination to follow Christ's leading and example without any reservation or hesitation. Let me introduce you to (or, perhaps more accurately, invite you to revisit them with me) some of my favorites.

Peter: oh, what an apt illustration of all humanity!

He was good, he was impetuous; he blew hot, he blew cold; he met soldiers coming for Jesus with a fierceness that ended in the slicing off of an ear, and a short time later he denied he even knew Christ three times.

Many of us see ourselves in Peter as he wavers from extreme to extreme in his faith. Everyone has had their ups and downs. The Matthew 14 story of Peter walking on water is a picture of who he was: He stepped out in faith and was able to walk to Jesus on water.

Then in typical Peter fashion, he soon took his eyes off Jesus and began to sink. He then cried out in his short burst of prayer, "Save me!" And Jesus saved him.

Peter did not seem to match his name's meaning: rock. He seemed more like a jellyfish floating whichever way the tide took him! Yet, from his jellyfish-like wavering, floating whichever way the current took him, he grew to solidify his love for Jesus.

Gradually and steadily, God was at work . . . transforming wishy-washy-Peter into Peter-the-Rock. Indeed, Jesus told Peter,

> *And I tell you, you are Peter, and on this rock I will build my church, and the gates of hell shall not prevail against it.*
>
> [Matthew 16:18. ESV]

He was martyred because of his steadfast, unwavering commitment to his faith in Jesus Christ. He grew from impetuous betrayer to a martyred apostle.

What changed Peter? Jesus saved him literally and spiritually. His faith grew. His confidence grew. He became firm, like the rock he was named for. Peter's story is important because it underscores the essential nature of confidence in God.

When Peter displayed his confidence, it was awesome. When he took his eyes off the One he placed his confidence in, he was weak. As Peter's eyes became more and more fixed on Jesus, his confidence and faith developed and grew. Confident eyes on Jesus, unwavering trust—that is the key to steadfastness.

Daniel: Headline—youth trusts God; miracles abound.

The story would make headlines today. It is riveting: young Hebrew men, thrown into a fiery furnace because they refused to bow to any other god but the one true God. It is familiar because it is so edge-of-the-seat and action-packed, it is a Sunday School favorite.

But the drama isn't the lesson within the account. The take-away point should be that Daniel and his friends' confidence was in God, no matter which way God decided to act. If rescue, fine; if not, also fine. Whatever the outcome, no other god would be worshipped. They trusted God to do what was best for them no matter what dangers were threatened:

> *Shadrach, Meshach, and Abednego replied to him, "King Nebuchadnezzar, we do not need to defend ourselves before you in this matter. If we are thrown into the blazing furnace, the God we serve is able to deliver us from Your Majesty's hand. But even if He does not, we want you to know, Your Majesty, that we will not serve your gods or worship the image of gold you have set up."*
>
> [Daniel 3:16-18. NIV]

God rewarded his unshaking faith when Daniel and the king were able to behold a fourth person "like the Son of God" [Daniel 3:25] emerge from the furnace with the unscathed trio: Shadrack, Meshack, and Abednego. Daniel expressed absolute faith in God again when he told King Darius that God would take care of him even though he did not follow the laws made by the governors and satraps of Babylon about praying to the king instead of the one true God.

Daniel had the confident attitude that if he honored God, God would protect him. He absolutely would not compromise and bow to anything or anyone but the one true God. With that attitude he was able to pray through an encounter with hungry lions instead of becoming their next meal [Daniel 6].

Abraham: unwavering trust in God when circumstances made no sense.

In Genesis 22, Abraham obeyed God and was ready to sacrifice his son. Yes, Isaac: the promised son he waited for until he was 100 years old. When God tested him, he showed unflinching faith that God would provide a lamb for the sacrifice, or would raise Isaac from the dead, confident to the point of raising the knife. And God provided the lamb.

Abraham wasn't perfect; he had made some of his own poor choices up to this time, but this was the same Abraham God had said He would make into a great nation. Abraham's response to this incident was to name the place "The LORD Will Provide" [verse 14] because Isaac had been spared, and a lamb had been provided as well as God reiterating the Genesis 12 covenant: blessing and nations. All of this because he had placed his confidence in God and obeyed Him to the point most would never go.

Nehemiah: bold for God, despite his circumstances.

Living the life of an exile, Nehemiah had mere slave-status in the court of King Artaxerxes of Persia. He served as the king's cupbearer, meaning he was the first to taste the king's food and drink in case someone tried to poison the king. As many servants in the king's palace were probably captive slaves, it would make sense that some of them hated being a slave in an enemy's land. The cupbearer, in those circumstances, was in the direct line of fire with so many who were being forced to serve.

It is reasonable to think some of the captives might want to see the king poisoned. However, Nehemiah served the king faithfully enough for the king to notice his sadness, and then the king cared enough about him to ask what was troubling him. Having heard about his homeland, Jerusalem in particular, being in ruins, he was saddened to hear that the walls of his beloved Jerusalem were broken down and the gates had been burned.

King Artaxerxes could have ignored Nehemiah's sad countenance. He could have dismissed anything he felt or wanted. But Nehemiah had evidently built a relationship with this foreign king he served, and Scripture reveals that the king listened and had enough compassion to allow him—a lowly servant of a captive people—to go home to repair the city that his country had rule over.

It took a lot of confidence for Nehemiah to presume to ask the king if he could go to Jerusalem and to rebuild what had been torn down during the captivity of the Israelites. His prayer [Nehemiah 1] is one of mourning and repentance. He believed a holy God would hear his petition. spoken in desperation and sadness.

He was afraid to ask, but didn't let that stop him. He was speaking to a king who had the power of life and death over him. And why would his captor care about the poor condition of a captured city? Yet, God used a sad face and a confident spirit to move a king to agree to let Nehemiah go home to the home of his father.

He showed further bravery when he asked the king to write letters to assure his safe passage through hostile territories on his way home. There were many problems along the way to getting the task completed, but notice how his confidence was strengthened within eighteen verses of the same chapter:

> *I was very much afraid. [and] The God of heaven will give us success.*
>
> [Nehemiah 2:2 (and) 2:20. NIV]

When Nehemiah tackled the enormous job of rebuilding the

walls and gates, he enlisted the help of everyone possible, from perfume makers to goldsmiths. They encountered opposition and ridicule, but he was confident he was doing what God wanted. He prayed—knowing he was despised and had a seemingly insurmountable task—and asked God to repay his opposition. He had a job to do and he kept working allowing God to fight the opposition for him.

When the wall was completed and the gates were in place, Nehemiah saw beyond the need for only physical restoration. He knew that worship to the one true God must be restored in Jerusalem.

Thus, God's Word was read, sins were confessed, the project was dedicated, and worship took place again—all because Nehemiah was confident that the living and powerful God who saw him through all the difficulties was the only God who deserved worship.

Elijah: the prophet who went over the top by mocking Baal's priests and pouring water in and around his sacrifice to God.

Elijah looked to heaven confidently and expectantly when he prayed for fire to fall on his dripping sacrifice, and to the surprise of all watching (as is continued to amaze incredulous readers today of I Kings 18) the fire fell.

How many of us are that confident God will work a miracle? It would have meant Elijah's life if he had failed. After all, it was one with a wet sacrifice against 450, but instead it meant the lives of 450 prophets of a false god who could not do or hear anything. He was only one against 450, yet he trusted in his God to do the impossible, and He did. God's people need a sense of desperation that leads to absolute confidence. The result can be, as it was in Elijah's day, "The Lord, He is God!"

I also learned from the lives of later-day heroes, from early days of modern missionary endeavors to those numbering among my contemporaries . . .

William Carey: esteemed pioneer missionary to India.

Fueled by a mutual love for my beloved homeland, my heart resonates with Carey's well-known quote,

> *Expect great things from God; attempt great things for God.*
>
> [From: his 1792 *"Deathless Sermon"*]

Carey expected God to move and work through him in India, and with that confident example, I confirmed I could too. William Carey went to India in 1793. He had been a pastor, and had founded the Baptist Missionary Society.

Convicted that Matthew 28 command to preach the Gospel "to all nations" was for contemporary Christians, not just Bible-time Christians, he felt compelled to go. Through a series of events he went to India with a medical doctor, John Thomas, who was returning to India for his second time.

Carey believed God's promises on which he based the earlier sermon:

> *Enlarge the place of your tent, and let them stretch out the curtains of your dwellings; do not spare; lengthen your cords, and strengthen your stakes. For you shall expand to the right and to the left, and your descendants will inherit the nations, and make the desolate cities inhabited.*
>
> [Isaiah 54:2-3. NKJV]

His first few years in India posed staggering hardships: managing an indigo plant, learning the Bengali language, beginning to translate the Bible into Bengali, founding a new missionary community, training indigenous pastors, losing his son Peter to dysentery, and the mental breakdown of his wife Dorothy. Through all these trials, there was not one convert to Christianity for seven years.

Shortly after that, his original partner, Dr. Thomas died. All the while, Carey continued to work on Bible translation and caring for a mentally unstable wife and their children. Dorothy died in 1807 and Carey married again the following year.

By that time, he was beginning the printing of the work he had been involved in translating. Then a fire broke out and his print shop retained costly damage along with losing translation work. It all sounds like very discouraging work, yet Carey never went back to his native England. He had faith in a God who he expected great things from—and got!

In his lifetime, the mission printed and distributed parts of, or whole Bibles, in 44 different languages and dialects. He founded Serampore College to train Indian pastors to pastor their own people; fought against the injustices of the caste system; began a horticulture society to promote farming practices. And, in spite of a separation from his original society, Carey continued to preach, teach and revise translations until he died in 1834, after over 40 years in India, confidently "expecting great things from God."

Jim Elliot . . .
Nate Saint . . .
Ed McCully . . .
Pete Fleming . . .
Roger Youderian: five who gave their all for the Gospel.

Not many may have known about these five men before they made worldwide news in January of 1956. But after they were martyred while attempting contact with an unreached tribe in an Ecuadoran rainforest, all of that changed. Their story captured hearts and minds—and changed lives. But it was not merely their story—the Gospel did it.

These men had prayed, made contact, given gifts, and felt assured they should make face-to-face contact. They were absolutely sure that they were to contact the Waorani (Huaorani) tribe, but paid with their lives on the bank of the remote Curaray River on a sand bar they had dubbed "Palm Beach."

Rachel Saint, Nate's sister, felt the death of her brother paralleled the sacrifice that Christ had made for the Waorani close to two thousand years previous to the death of the five missionaries. Elisabeth Elliot, Jim's wife, and Rachel Saint were so confident in God's leading that they went back to minister to and evangelize the very tribe that had killed their loved ones.

Steve Saint, Nate's son, also spent much of his life with the same people, coming to love them, and he took as a substitute father for the one he grew up without, one of the very band that had speared his father to death. Steve's 2004 documentary, *Beyond the Gates of Splendor*, underscores two points:

1. These tragic deaths of five young men—who left wives, children, and other loved ones behind—were not an accident.

2. Rather, the heartbreak that came from loss of physical lives was used to God's glory to bring the Gospel to the Waoranis. The end result was salvation and eternal life for hundreds of Waorani people.

They are still in the Ecuadorian jungle today, but they no longer practice the cruelties prevalent in their lives over 50 years ago that had killed and enslaved so many of them. Jesus Christ made the difference because five brave men trusted, went, paid the price, and became the catalyst for changing that entire tribe for the Kingdom.

George Mueller: prayer warrior who pounded on heaven's door.

Another figure in the history of missions, Mueller built orphanages and then cared for the children he brought there, literally with prayer. Only prayer—confident, trusting prayer.

He grew up in Germany in the early 1800s and was quite a scoundrel in his early years. He looked at Christians as a source of ridicule, so when he was invited to a Bible study, he went for the fun of making fun. To his amazement, he liked it because he encountered people who were genuine in their faith. Shortly after this, he became a Christian, losing all his old friends he had partied with before, and gaining a desire to become, of all things: a missionary.

Mueller's father was not pleased that George desired such a life of poverty; he refused to pay for any more schooling. Even without his father's support, the son went to school to study for his new-found passion, not knowing how he would pay his tuition.

At school he knelt to pray about his dilemma, and within an hour he was offered a tutoring job that would pay for his schooling. That established prayer as the vital force in his life that was the source of all he accomplished in life.

After finishing his education, he left Germany to be a missionary in England, and became a pastor there. Before long in his ministry, he became incensed at the inequality within the first church he was called to pastor. His salary was to be paid from revenue derived from the rental of front-row pews for rich church goers. The poor had to sit in the back in less desirable seats. If this congregation wanted him as pastor, he told them, this practice had to stop. It did, but he still refused to draw a salary.

Like Mother Teresa would do years later, Mueller trusted God to provide for every need. He and his family never missed a meal or rent payment.

When George walked the streets seeing needs, he began to feel God calling him to another occupation because of the needy children he encountered on his walks. The result was the founding of an orphanage which would eventually provide care for 10,000 children. Literally everything provided came through prayer: the building, all food, clothing, the staff, the furniture, and the Bible he gave every orphan who eventually left his care.

David Livingstone: unorthodox, yes, but single-minded for God.

This Scotsman considered whatever occupation he did during his 60 years of life—doctor; shooting an animal for meat for those helping him; being an explorer; or "conventional" missionary—as serving Christ. To Livingstone, every act was serving Christ.

He was interested in going to places no missionary had ever been, and first started serving in South Africa. His nonconformist behavior and approach to living in Africa was anything but conventional. In his attempt to make a road for missionaries to travel into "regions beyond" so they could take the Gospel to people who had never heard the name of Jesus, he behaved in ways unappreciated and unexpected.

A rather eccentric man, Livingstone had trouble getting along with fellow workers and others he encountered because he felt they were being very colonial in their approach to reaching the lost. He also ran into conflict with his mission society because they felt he was doing things, like exploring, that distracted from his mission work.

So, while often at odds with the people most like him in nationality and occupation, he got along well with the Africans he served with more understanding and respect than any missionary had before. He especially hated the slave trade and despicable behavior of the slavers he saw firsthand, and wanted it cut off at the source before Africans were shipped to the West, meaning mainly the Americas.

On one trip up the Nile after his wife's death, he simply disappeared into the still uncharted African interior. During his time away living within the tribes, he was very sick and yet managed to read the Bible through four times and kept detailed journals, the transcripts of these can still be read.

An American journalist, Henry Stanley, later "found" the missing Livingstone and gave rise to the famed "Dr. Livingstone, I presume?" quote, which he inquired of the only European within thousands of miles! Written about and treated as a hero on his brief visits back to Britain, (he also traveled to other countries on humanitarian and intellectual pursuits, including India) Livingstone scorned reports of his heroism and sacrifice. His recorded response was,

> Can that be called a sacrifice which is simply paid back as a small part of a great debt owing to our God, which we can never repay? Away with the word in such a view and with such a thought: it is emphatically no sacrifice. Say rather it is a privilege. Anxiety, sickness, suffering, or danger now and then with a foregoing of the common conveniences and charities of this life, may make us pause and cause the spirit to waver and the soul

> to sink; but let this only be for a moment. All these are nothing when compared with the glory which shall be revealed in and for us. I never made a sacrifice.
>
> [From: Speech at Cambridge University in 1857]

Livingstone made Victoria Falls known to the world and enabled map makers to help travelers reach remote African tribes, but he himself cared nothing for the comforts of civilized life. His dogged determination to live with the Africans showed his burning desire to make God's Word known "up close and personal" to those who knew it not.

Left to his own devices, he confidently disappeared into that cause: making Christ known in tribes where Jesus had never been named. He didn't think of his disappearance as leaving "all." It was what he knew God wanted him to devote the remaining of his life to, and he needed nothing other than the freedom to go on his terms and tell about Jesus.

Ravi Zacharias: a man with unswerving confidence in God.

I first heard this thought-provoking evangelist and apologist speak in our shared homeland soon after my conversion. One sermon he preached prompted me to seek a deeper walk with Christ. Dr. Zacharias, who is also a TEDS alumnus, uses his confidence in what he has learned from God and His Word to be a proponent of Truth to this generation.

A noted and sought after speaker, he is unafraid of challenges from believers in false religions, and uses his command of Scripture to answer questions and doubts. His ability to speak truth with confidence and hia keen intellect has earned the respect of virtually everyone, including critics. Consider his organization's mission and vison statements:

> The primary mission of Ravi Zacharias International Ministries is to reach and challenge those who shape the

ideas of a culture with the credibility of the Gospel of Jesus Christ. Distinctive in its strong evangelistic and apologetic foundation, the ministry of RZIM is intended to touch both the heart and the intellect of the thinkers and influencers of society through the support of the visionary leadership of Ravi Zacharias.

Our vision is to build a team with a fivefold thrust of evangelism, apologetics, spiritual disciplines, training, and humanitarian support so that the mandate of I Peter 3:15 might be fulfilled: to set apart Christ in our hearts as Lord and always be prepared to give a reason for the hope that is within us, with gentleness and respect, all for the glory of God.

[From: rzim.org, the ministry's website]

That says it all. Ravi depends on God in whom he has all confidence to reach the world for the glory of God. The components of Kingdom leadership are right there.

Ruth Tucker: former TEDS missiology and church history teacher.

She considers the stories of missionaries throughout history to be portrayals of unusual confidence in God's leading and direction as He guides His followers to take the Gospel to all peoples everywhere. One of those accounts Tucker records is of Vibia Perpetua, whose story has had a great influence on her life.

Vibia lived in the third century during the Roman persecution of Christians. She was a believer and was arrested for the crime of letting it be known her trust and confidence was in Jesus as Savior. Her father begged her to deny Christ and be freed from prison. He pleaded, bringing her child to see her, begging Vibia to give up and to come home to live with them.

Vibia replied, "Be gone from me, enemies of God, for I know you not!" She refused by turning her back on her beloved family rather than deny Jesus. She was then put in a place to be tortured by a bear, leopard, and wild boar. Even after this agony, she refused to deny Christ. Her life ended with beheading.

What confidence Vibia had to have in the face of such pressure! She had to know, beyond any shadow of a doubt, that she was faced with going to see Jesus. Tucker cannot imagine any of Vibia's scenario: the imprisonment, the torture, the decision to choose between her Savior and death, or her family. But this story Tucker includes in her book, From Jerusalem to Irian Jaya, spurs her to not be complacent or take for granted that she has not had to defend her faith in such a fashion.

Tucker ponders ". . .whether I would show similar unwavering faith in Jesus and trust in the unshakable hope I have in Him." She admits her need for confidence should she face such extreme challenge.

Safety and lack of persecution in our society does not always give us a resolute confidence, but a sure confidence is essential to Kingdom leadership. We are defeated before we begin if we do not have an unshakable confidence in the King for Whom we are leading.

Christians around the world are being persecuted right now for their faith. It makes one wonder if there is a need to suffer persecutions in order to have that unswerving, absolute faith in Christ. Those who follow Christ will endure sufferings [II Timothy 3:12].

To be a Kingdom-style leader requires following our Lord confidently. Not just when it is easy. However, I firmly believe the walk with Christ, and the confidence in Him does become easier as love for Him grows. A deepening relationship with Jesus builds confidence, and develops an even greater determination to follow Jesus without reservation.

CHAPTER 12

Spouse Shares the Vision

A spouse who shares the vision of Kingdom work is vital to fulfill a God-sized vision in order to reflect the relationship between Christ and the Church in this world. Not all are called to be married [implied in I Corinthians 7:1] but having a partner who brings a shared vision of ministry to a marriage is vital to fulfill a God-sized vision.

I am so blessed to have Mony. From the depths of my heart, I say: if that woman had not been willing to join with me in this mission, it would have been difficult. To accomplish great things, anyone who is married needs a good life partner. Mine is an amazing woman!

Most girls--Indian or American—want to be around their parents, siblings, cousins, friends. Mony was different. She told me she would go wherever I went. Although we were married in India, Mony spent most of her growing up years in New York where much of her family still resides today.

I say affectionately that Mony has never asked me for anything. She spent many years living in a small apartment, never asking for a house. Many times, we kept up to five or six pastors with only two bedrooms and one bathroom. Mony would uncomplainingly fix meals and care for our guests. A house was not a priority for us, and Mony never asked or complained, though when visitors from India came in the early days, they would ask me why we were living in that manner!

If Mony had complained every time I came in from the field, I would have been a struggling leader and would not have had any peace, but she never did. She grew up with people telling her she would be a missionary in North India someday. Those prophetic words seemed to be untrue as she married me: a trained accountant.

But God had a plan. God's plan brought me the gift of Mony, and I brought both of us to share in the dream to minister together, to plant churches in every state in India.

A leader's effectiveness is hampered if the husband or wife does not share in the vision for the marriage as well as for ministry. Within marriage, communicating the hopes and visions for how the spouses are going to fulfill God's plan for their life together is vital to the life and health of a marriage and any ministry.

Conflict and discord can ruin unity, and will be detrimental to ministry and marriage. With Christians, when the act of getting married combines two into one, it means everything done together or separately must be for the conjoined good of the couple, and always to honor the Lord. It is another way of interpreting the old saying, "What's good for the goose is good for the gander."

It doesn't mean that a woman will want to or can do all a man does, and vice versa. But it does mean when there is Kingdom vision involved, it is for both partners. That makes it of primary importance to get together on God's plan and to set mutual goals to carry that plan out. Prayer is going to help in this journey of bringing a couple together in purpose and unity.

Whether married or single, people are often like little children learning to share toys. Watch little ones as they play. When there is a question of "mine versus yours," the stance is universal: the object and attitude is clutched closely to the chest as a means to let the other person know the property belongs to the one doing the clutching.

It's not a pretty picture, is it? Parents often have a hard time guiding children to learn how to share or to relinquish what they don't want to share. It is unnatural to share anything unless we view everything as God's, with the understanding that God shares everything we hold. Nothing is ours. It is all His but, like a child's selfish attitude, this premise is too often rejected.

People grasp and challenge God's ownership with selfish attitudes, which do not acknowledge that we "own" nothing. Releasing perceived ownership is crucial, whether it be clinging to ambitions, plans, or possessions. We must develop the attitude that we are merely caretaking whatever God gives us and allows to be within the realm of our control.

Just as it has been said in a previous chapter that a Kingdom leader must enjoy credibility at home within the family members, the same manner of unity within a shared vision must be incubated in the marriage through prayer and togetherness in purpose and goals.

Comparing the selfish child mentality to marriage shows how deeply God needs to be entrenched in a marriage. Those clutching attitudes of selfishness need to give way to embracing attitudes of selflessness, all enabled by a God who wants to bathe marriage in His grace.

When, in God's will, a leader has such a spouse, this relationship will enhance ministry work in ways that can only be attributed to God's grace. A like-minded spouse is someone to pray and to dream with, and thus forge ahead together.

The spouse can be the island of relief when there are difficulties. The spouse will be right alongside in times when needed or will keep the home and family going when travel or other duties call one away from home. Without such a spousal relationship, ministry can be crippled.

Kingdom work can grind to a halt if spouses do not share in vision and purpose in life and ministry. That does not mean that spouses will think exactly alike. In fact, God in His wisdom often puts people with different ideas and approaches together for the express purpose of filling in gaps each spouse has. God doesn't expect us to find the perfect-fitting spouse, but wants to help us find the spouse who will make us more than we can be by ourselves.

Love each other as Christ loves the Church, and find the perfection so many seek but never find. It isn't about a perfect spouse, it's all about a perfect God, and a couple serving Him together.

When it came time that I felt it was time to marry, I asked God for a wife who would share ministry with me. I got all I asked God for and more! Mony is a gift from God to be my life- and ministry-partner of blessing. Her own dreams of ministry were also fulfilled in marrying me, because she is a Godly woman who loved the Lord.

From the very beginning, Mony was my staunchest supporter and constant encourager. She was willing to leave her family in New York, where they had immigrated from India in 1979 when she was 14, to follow me halfway across the United States to seminary in Illinois, and as we began to lay the groundwork for what would become RIMI in the United States and MI in India.

She worked hard, prayed hard, and she was the exact companion of God's choosing for me. During the times I go to India without Mony, she tends the home fires near Chicago. She adapted to life with me by working hard to support me during the rigors of graduate school; kept (and keeps) numerous ministry partners in our home; has entertained many guests and cooked multiple meals, and often has been right alongside me on the travels, as well.

She continues to support every facet of ministry, and is a vital part of it. In fact, RIMI staff in the States say, "Without Mony, there is no Saji."

Mony has always willingly spent periods of time at home caring for our daughter, Maryann, and maintaining jobs—all to further the advance of the Gospel, which is what our shared mission is all about.

From early on, during the birth pangs of my vision for RIMI and our work establishing MI, Mony was a constant support in prayer; in fasting; tending to all the things that still had to be done to maintain a Christian household where we could be at home, and to provide a refuge where God is honored above all else.

My essential concepts for a marriage relationship which honors God and enhances Kingdom leadership in ministry are:

- Treasure God's never-failing grace
- Praying together
- Dreaming together
- Willingly sacrificing for one another
- Considering God and His plan first
- Using our complimentary, yet diverse gifts
- Covenanting to never mention the word "divorce".

These are the central traits Mony and I have focused on and fostered in our marriage to remain compatible as we pursue God together.

I've heard my friend and classmate from our TEDS days, Jeff Whitt, say in reference to the Lukos marriage and relationship, "It was clear then as it is now, that Saji is a man of tremendous passion and of love for souls, and he and Mony both are and were willing to make great sacrifices to reach the peoples of India with the Gospel."

It all boils down to my passion shaping our marriage, and how Mony has shared that with me since our very first days together.

God's Grace

A solid marriage with a shared vision for ministry and mission is a gracious gift of God's grace and mercy. God continues to give grace to strengthen marriage and the passions for serving God that are shared in the family as well as shared ministry.

Noted author and motivational speaker Zig Ziglar wisely said,

> Many marriages would be better if the husband and the wife clearly understood that they are on the same side.

Sadly, this is true about too many marriages, yet God chose marriage to be a picture of His love for humankind. So marriage is a gift of God's grace, which should be treasured, showing the gift of grace toward one another. If we incubate the gift of grace, it grows and produces more and more grace. When a couple shows grace to one another, they can easily be gracious to others, as well.

Pray Together

There is nothing that can bind and solidify a marriage more than the act of praying together with a mutual passion to see ministry furthered and nurtured. The shared prayers of a married couple can be effective in the struggles and triumphs of ministry, but can also serve to bless the union and the work the couple shares.

For even if only one is directly involved in ministry, both can share in the burden of care for the work to be accomplished.

Prayers become a time of sharing before the Lord that surpasses any conversations as the Lord opens both hearts before His throne.

In our marriage, prayer is of utmost importance. We prayed about finding each other, then continued together as God brought us into marriage, and prayer continues to be of absolute necessity. During our first six years of marriage, there were many changes and moves.

Ministries were birthed; countless miles were traveled; education was furthered. We worked hard. We always had each other and that vital prayer link even if travel kept us apart for periods of time. However, we had one heartbreak: no child.

We waited for our union in marriage to bring about a baby, but none came. We went to God, and asked many others to go to God on our behalf, asking for a child. The desire did not go away; we wanted a child.

Additionally, this was a hard thing culturally because in India it is expected for a couple to produce a child within the first couple years of marriage. The Indian grandparents felt the void and were disappointed, as well. However, Mony especially bore the brunt of childlessness because she felt responsible, even though she knew better.

She knew the old cultural traditions from her Indian heritage, and could not help but feel especially saddened by our childless state. Mony recalled the prophecy of a Pastor Thomas she had heard at an uncle's New York church during her teen years.

The pastor had told her that when she was 21 her life would take a new direction, and that she would be involved in a ministry known throughout the world.

When Mony was 21, she married me. Toward the end of 1992, we met up with Pastor Thomas again at a prayer meeting we attended at the home of mutual friends. At that prayer meeting, Pastor Thomas and his wife laid hands on Mony and prayed, rebuking Satan's schemes to leave us without a future generation.

A few months later Mony discovered she was pregnant, at long last, during a trip back to India. I immediately phoned my mother-in-law in New York with the news, and she shared that they had been praying and God had confirmed that Mony would have a child. Our faithful, fervent prayers and those of family and friends were answered. We were ecstatic at the birth of our daughter Maryann a few months later in 1993.

Dream together

When a couple shares a vision for ministry, they can openly dream both in conversation and through prayer what God could accomplish through their marriage. Once God has joined a man and woman together, He truly makes them one—in body, in heart, in mind, in dreams for the future of their involvement in His Kingdom.

It is natural for couples to dream together when they are engaged and planning to get married. All is focused on the future they face together.

But sometimes that dreaming together gets set aside as jobs and homemaking and life, in general, encroaches on the newness of that first envisioning the future together. It is important to keep that sense of a shared dream alive, or if it is dead, resurrect it.

That sense of awe in seeing God's plan in place before it comes about should not be lost. God wants to be a supernatural component in a couples lives and marriage because He actually knows what is in store. Couples can look forward to God's plan and work and presence in their lives knowing He will always have their best in mind.

Never lose that sense of God's holiness and supreme direction that is beyond anything we can achieve, except through His divine intervention. Expect God's leading to be ever present in life and marriage. It is important to dream together and to have that sense of future work God is going to be doing in and through the marriage partners as a couple. Let Him lead shared dreams.

Sacrifice for One Another

Committed spouses truly think of themselves as one, not separate. Each one thinks more highly of the other than self. Thoughts, wishes, and prayers for the other—all are for the best, and brings each partner to a place of doing all that is possible to make mutual dreams come true.

Likewise, committed spouses willing sacrifice for the good of their marriage and marriage partner. It is at the heart of a Christian marriage that honors God to sacrifice self for the sake of spouse and marriage and of ministry.

French literature critic, Charles Du Bos says,

> The important thing is this: to be able at any moment to sacrifice what we are for what we could become.
>
> [From: *Approximations*]

This comes from a secular source, but is good advice. The reality of honoring God who brought you together in marriage, involves honoring one another within that marriage. Self is never first.

Striving for a holy, God-honoring marriage must be an on-going goal. Likewise, a ministry team with a Kingdom-style leader operates much like a good marriage: always striving to be better. In marriage and ministry always striving to be more of what God wants you to be is a striving for holiness in every part of life, whether personal- or ministry-related. It is an ever present attitude of a partnership of "us" and never "me."

Darlene Schacht gives excellent advice for putting Christ at the center of our marriages. If the words are applied either to leadership qualities or to a good marriage, it is sound and solid wisdom:

> Marriage is a thousand little things . . . It's giving up your right to be right in the heat of an argument. It's forgiving another when they let you down. It's loving someone enough to step down so they can shine. It's friendship. It's being a cheerleader and trusted confidant. It's a place of forgiveness that welcomes one home, and arms they can run to in the midst of a storm. It's grace.
> [From: *Time-Warp Wife*]

Change the words in just a few places, and it can relate to how a Kingdom leader views those he or she works with. The words are wise counsel in almost any circumstance.

Anyone who treats a spouse or ministry partner in that way will most surely be blessed by God's pleasure, as well as the pleasure of the people involved. Jesus used marriage as an analogy of Christ and the Church, and Ephesians 5:25 tells husbands to love their wives as Christ loved the Church. Christ's love was a sacrificial love that went to the extreme of giving His life on the cross for the world so those in the Church might have life.

Consider God above Everything

God's Word says He is a jealous God [Exodus 20:5]. He wants the part of His creation—we, who He made in His image—to love Him unreservedly, because love was what He created as, to quote Francis Chan: the "catalyst of all Godly actions."

God created love. He is the author of love we give anyone else; without Him there is no love. He wants us to place Him first in our affections. Many verses throughout the Bible, adMonysh us to love God above all else. Jesus quoted this Old Testament passage twice [Luke 10:27; Matthew 22:37]:

> *Love the LORD your God with all your heart and with all your soul and with all your strength.*
> [Deuteronomy 6:5. NIV]

A good, solid Christian marriage can put God first and yet, because of the regard God has for this union He created, still allow spouses to love each other exclusively and hold one another in highest regard—making this a double benefit to both a relationship with God and between the human partners.

Putting God first draws a couple closer in love as their shared allegiance to Christ melds them together as nothing else can. Pleasing God together brings a married couple even closer together.

To love God above everything, to want His direction and plan worked out in your marriage, to additionally serve in ministry together—it is all pleasing to God. Serving your spouse with a servant's heart, allows you to serve others with a servant's heart. A servant's heart is what a Kingdom leader must have.

Thus, a successful Christian union to a spouse who leads home, family, and marriage with Godly servanthood, will be be God-pleasing in leadership and in the home. It cannot be accomplished unless God is first in the home, the family, and the marriage. Every consideration for one another is a consideration for God's Kingdom because a committed marriage brings honor and glory to God.

Gifts Complement

God made each of us different from all others for a reason. Spouses can complement one another in marriage. Where one is weak, the other spouse may have traits of strength. Where one is very cerebral, the other can be down to earth and practical. Even in temperament, one can be up while the other is down.

The dichotomy of two people, each operating within his and her own particular personality and gifting; contribute to the making of a perfect whole. This is one of God's great mysteries and gifts to the individual man and woman joined together in marriage.

Divorce Should Never Be Considered!

God hates divorce [Malachi 2:16]. He clearly states in the Bible that divorce is a result of hardness of hearts [Matthew 19:8].

In this current age of "throw away" marriages and appallingly high divorce rates even within the Christian community, it is a wonderful testimony to the world when a couple has long-lasting marital permanence. Such a union becomes an example of utter, absolute commitment in a day of so many shattered matriMonyal dreams.

The marriage vows of today often omit—in heart, if not in fact—the ideals of "for better or worse" and "'til death do us part." It can be concluded that too few spouses view their spouses—and their marriage—as a gift of God's grace.

Interestingly, it has long been believed that Christian marriages have had as high failure rate as the rest of the world.

In the world at large, there is a reported 50-percent divorce rate. But Harvard-educated researcher, Shaunti Feldhahn, conducted an eight-year research project on the divorce rates of married couples who are part of a church. She learned that couples who attend church have a 15- to 20-percent lower rate of marriage failure. Feldhahn states,

> People need to know this. People need to be able to look around the average congregation and say, "You know what, most of these people will have strong and happy marriages for a lifetime. Doing what God says matters." This is a big deal to know.
>
> [From: *The Good News about Marriage*. Quoted by Paul Strand, CBN News Washington correspondent]

Strand further reports,

> For religious believers, if they'll be attentive to practice their faith with their spouse, they can almost double their odds of avoiding divorce.

During this CBN program, Strand also quoted Angel H. Davis, licensed Clinical Social Worker and Board-Certified professional Christian counselor. He credits Davis with saying,

> When you have something like a statistic like 50-percent, it gives you the option. It becomes an option in your mind.

Davis goes on to say that this information could go a long way toward erasing the doubt that Christianity makes no difference. This information can do two things:

1. It can show that the world's view of divorce being universal is damaging to marriages because it makes it an option to take if God, the Church, and

following Christ makes no difference. This lie robs the institution of marriage of the important quality of hope.

2. If the option of divorce is taken away, and Christian marriage is looked at as a permanent institution, the world can learn that Christ does make a positive difference in marriage.

In any case, divorce is damaging, does not honor God, is not something He looks at with favor, and should not be an option. The view the world has on divorce makes it more acceptable even to Christians, and to not give the Church the credit it deserves for preserving marriage, is devastating.

To believe divorce is *the answer* is to let Satan's lie supplant truth. Divorce has been perpetuated against the God-given institution of marriage. It hurts families and damages ministries. Christians should do all that can be done to change the skewed viewpoint of the world. It is imperative that the word "divorce" should never be in a married couple's conversations or considerations.

And it needs to be known that God makes all the difference in the world. Christians need to take back the reputation of Christian marriage. Christ needs to be present in our marriages. He needs to be the head of our homes. With Him, we can have Kingdom-honoring marriages.

> *Though one may be overpowered, two can defend themselves. A cord of three strands is not quickly broken.*
> [Ecclesiastes 4:12. NIV]

Christ needs to be that third strand in a marriage. Godly Kingdom-style leadership commands it.

Early in our marriage, Mony and I vowed to one another that the word "divorce" would never be in our dictionary. I firmly believe my Godly wife is a gift from God, an answer to fervent prayer, and brought about through obedience and yielding to God's perfect plan for my life.

With God answering my requests completely with Mony, I have, since our wedding day, regarded our commitment to one another as permanent. I vowed before God that I will love her until death parts us.

Mony, raised in a Christian family that honored the cultural Indian traditions, made her vows to me with equal fervency. The faithfulness lived out in our lives to God and one another has been a Godly testimony to the world, and makes my Kingdom-style leadership a model that works.

As Francis Chan succinctly puts it,

> Public passion should never exceed private devotion.
>
> [From: *"Why It's So Easy for Leaders to Fake it,"* published on: churchleaders.com]

I have been a passionate follower of Jesus since I gave my heart to Christ as a young man. My love for Jesus only grows. I live a life of fervent servant leadership in my home and in the ministries I have founded. How? God did it all.

Great devotion to God allows a great God to do great things. My utmost wish is that these leadership lessons will bring insight, challenge, blessing, and rethinking for your life and ministry for God's Kingdom.

Application Questions for "Lessons Learned on Kingdom Leadership"

Chapter One: Begin with Christ

1. Search your memory and use your imagination to describe how you might be different today if you had not been transformed by faith in Jesus Christ. What desires, thoughts, ambitions, and tendencies might be driving your decisions and leadership? What leadership model do you think you would be following if you had not begun with Christ?

2. Write out your own transformation story. Describe what you experienced before you responded to the Gospel and how following Jesus has made a difference. What immediate changes were evident in your life? What other changes happened later in your Christian experiences? How do these changes affect your concept of helping other people?

3. How does remembering how you were changed by the Gospel awaken gratitude for the transforming power of God? What problems in other people's lives seem obvious to you because of your own past? How has God been equipping you through your own growth to help others? Do you think God could use you in specific ways because of the path of your life so far?

4. Have you realized that you are important to God? How does this affect the way you view your life and purpose? How does it affect the way you view other people and their needs? Have other people become more important to you because of knowing they are important to God? Does this perspective discourage you? Or, does it make you want to help?

5. Most leaders in the world are willing to fight, manipulate, deceive, compromise, and assert in order to gain a position

of influence and control over others. How is Jesus' servant leadership different from the world's way? Are you in some ways repulsed by Jesus' example, preferring what seems to be more successful in the world's example? How does the Gospel itself empower you to reject the world's way and follow the path of servant leadership?

Chapter Two: Establish Credibility at Home

1. Are there issues you still have with your parents or siblings or extended family that you need to clear up? Before you proceed with leadership outside your home, rebuild credibility and integrity with your family that may have been damaged by your past actions and attitudes.

2. Are your family members believers in Jesus? If not, have you taken leadership steps to wisely and lovingly share the Gospel with them? Are you faithfully praying for their salvation and maturity in Christ? Depending on the family dynamics, this may be a harder task than ministering to strangers, but it should be a priority for your exercise of spiritual leadership.

3. If you are married, did you choose your partner on the basis of romantic feelings, personal attraction, and desire? Or, on the basis of teamwork and partnership in serving the Lord? Marriage has been described as a "yoke" that harnesses two animals together to pull a wagon or a plow. The yoke keeps the animals close to each other, but what is important is that they are going in the same direction, combining their abilities and energy for the same task, and submitting to the same Master.

4. Sit down with your spouse and review (or work on for the first time) what God might want you to pull together as a team. Start with prayer for God's guidance and take time for honest and open discussion. Don't pressure each other, but work together to define specifically what you think God had in mind for you as a family. What do you believe God has called

you to? How has God equipped you through gifts, abilities, experiences, and lessons learned? What inescapable longing has he placed in your hearts? What needs are you most aware of in people that you see and know? Do you have a life verse that gives direction to your efforts? When the world and all that is in the world has passed away, what will you have left to present to the Lord?

5. After you have defined the overall purpose of your ministry as a family, work out the strategies that make the most sense, based on the individual gifts and strengths of each family member. How are you different in ways that complement each other? How can you support each other in the challenges caused by weaknesses or negative tendencies? In what ways do you need to protect against taking advantage of each other or manipulation to your human will?

Chapter Three: Identify your Destiny

1. Have you settled once-for-all that you will not waste your life pursuing what the world has to offer (material goods, physical desires, personal pride)? All these will pass away. Have you determined instead that you will use whatever worldly possessions or advantages you gain to invest in eternal values?

2. Verify (or discover for the first time) what spiritual gifts you have from God. Study the lists in Romans 12 and I Corinthians 12 for guidance. God always equips his people for the destiny to which he calls them.

3. Take time to walk through the five purposes listed in this chapter, taken from The Purpose Driven Life. If you are married, do it as a couple. Write down your responses so you have a working document to guide your sense of calling.

4. Do you have an inescapable passion for your life? What

is your "sweet spot" of ministry? What activities give you the greatest satisfaction, confidence, and expectation of lasting fruit? Do you have a hero or role model you deeply admire and aspire to be like? These might be God's way of prompting you towards what he is calling you to.

5. What evils and problems in the world cause you to weep or to become angry? Do you have a burden for certain people that keeps you awake at night? Are your mind and your emotions tuned in to a specific wrong that you want to see corrected? This might be God's invitation to give kingdom leadership in addressing these situations.

Chapter Four: Pray Specifically

1. Have you taken time to wait on the Lord through prayer, fasting, and seeking God? Ask a group of trusted, godly family members, friends, and mentors to join you in seeking confirmation of what you believe God has called you to do. Seek God's guidance and power on your vision, freely admitting your desperate need of God to make it happen.

2. Leadership carries with it many temptations. Our efforts to serve God and people can be sidetracked in so many ways. Establish accountability relationships that will be ongoing. Make sure your accountability is based on prayer. Pray with your partners and your family for Christ-like humility and a servant's heart. Pray for God's guidance to take precedence over human understanding. Pray for his supernatural power to secure eternal results.

3. Are you content to attempt only what you believe you can accomplish with known resources? Or, is there an element of faith at work? What do you want to see happen that will certainly fail unless God provides what only he can do?

4. Can you handle unanswered prayers? Can you live with

answers to your prayers that are different from what you hoped for? Remember to pray, "Thy kingdom come, Thy will be done." Beware of being so focused on your vision of your destiny that you become frustrated or discouraged when God tries to redirect you by his wisdom.

5. Make time in your schedule and make a priority decision in your life to cultivate prayer as the backbone of ministry. Don't settle for prayer as a mere formality for public approval. Don't settle for prayer as a last resort in emergency situations. Make prayer the starting point for every plan, decision, policy, and attitude.

Chapter Five: Dream a God-Sized Vision

1. Have you taken extended time to seek God in prayer and fasting so that he can refine, correct, and flesh out your vision for ministry? Ask your family, mentors, and close associates to join you as you lay out your tentative plans before the Lord. Take time to listen to the Holy Spirit after you describe each part of your vision in specific detail.

2. Work through the six component questions listed in this chapter: Is it from God? Is every facet for his glory? Will it result in transformation? Is it based on the greatness of God? Is it presented to others with clarity? Do I communicate it with passion?

3. Has God directed you to Biblical principles that provide foundation for your vision? You should be able to take a key Bible verse as the summary statement of your ministry. Be careful that it is not a verse taken out of context, but supported by clear teaching from various passages of Scripture.

4. What evidence of brokenness in individual people or in society's problems supports the urgency of you vision? Have you actually studied the needs through research and

observation to know that your proposed ministry will address and transform the damage done by sin? Define how your work will contribute to the Kingdom of God.

5. Are you hearing confirmation from others as you share your vision? Do people who are marked by courageous faith affirm you in pursuing your goals? Do people who are more practical-minded shake their heads or offer cautions about being realistic (in terms of human possibilities and limited resources)? A God-sized vision should draw both kinds of response.

Chapter Six: Faithful in the Little Things

1. As you wait for the development of your vision into a significant life-changing ministry, do you chafe under the sense of wasting your time in less important duties? Or, do you have a responsible commitment to doing with excellence the tasks you now have as unto the Lord? Now is the time to establish a pattern of faithfulness, doing your best, and seeing God's glory in everything.

2. Have you made a commitment to keep all your own assessments of success or failure tentative, waiting for the final evaluation to be determined by God himself? Can you accept thanks and praise graciously without becoming overly concerned about the opinions of others?

3. Can you receive criticism and negative comments with similar grace, drawing benefit from them while continuing to do your work faithfully to the Lord? Is it possible that God is using unqualified critics to call your attention to areas in which he wants to give you growth? Let God and his word provide the authoritative correction, but be willing to accept a signal to check things out from any source.

4. Examine yourself and ask close friends to be brutally honest with you about any indications of laziness in your life.

Are you excusing a lack of diligence or focus by blaming your background or upbringing? Does carelessness in little things reveal attitudes of pride, self-centeredness, or entitlement? If so, treat these as potential destroyers of your vision and ministry. Make a major effort through Bible study, prayer, accountability, and dependence on the Holy Spirit to correct these sins.

5. Are you working on a strategy to get from where you are now to where you hope to end up? We are called by a God-sized vision, but that vision must be built with small steps. Faithfulness in little things means having a plan and patience to build a solid foundation, treating the details with integrity, and allowing God to give the increase.

Chapter Seven: Build Your Team

1. Is your personality suited to energetic action, able to do the work of ten people? Consider your high energy, passion, and willingness to work hard as gifts from God. Don't compromise that equipping and don't stop being a leader. But, take time to develop a strategy for investing your energy wisely in developing other people. No one can "sell" your vision, recruit a team of ministry, and refresh the vision like you can.

2. How are you multiplying your Kingdom work? Have you defined the type of people you are looking for to join you in your ministry? What spiritual gifts, character traits, commitments to God, and freedom from bondage would you like to see in your coworkers? Do you believe that God is raising up people with the heart for what drives you? Do you have confidence in the work of the Holy Spirit in other people's hearts to equip them to come alongside you? Are you actively praying for God to bring such people into your life?

3. How fragile is you own ego? Would you be threatened by a fellow minister who seemed to have more success than

you do (as King Saul was threatened by David)? Bring this potential hindrance before the Lord in prayer, asking for a spirit of humility and a servant's heart. Renew your commitment to the Kingdom of God that is more important than your desire to receive personal acclaim. As you build your team, look for people who are sensitive to the Lord, people willing to sacrifice for the Kingdom, people whom God can use in mighty ways.

4. You cannot do all the work of the ministry. God doesn't intend that you do. What priority are you giving to the work of recruiting and equipping your team? Is asking God to raise up people to work alongside you number 30 on your prayer list? Or, is it closer to the top?

5. Have you begun thinking of a plan of succession? You probably expect the ministry you lead to outlive you. Who will take over when you are unable to continue as its leader? Can this long-range question be part of your team building?

Chapter Eight: Risk Your Life for Others

1. Are you able to see undeveloped potential? Not everyone can. Can you look at a bird's egg and visualize the full-grown bird that will eventually come from it? Can you spot a diamond in the rough? Your team will not be built totally from people who are fully mature and successful when you first meet them. Are you prepared to patiently guide team members in their growth? Can you help them to overcome sinful patterns, develop their gifts, refine their understanding of the ministry, and become leaders themselves?

2. Mistakes by your fellow workers obviously can harm the ministry--and can make you look bad. No one is comfortable when such things happen. Are you willing to take that risk? Do you see this potential damage as part of leaving your nets to follow Jesus? Are you able to fully turn over responsibility and all its risks to those you work with? Are you willing to take the

risks Jesus took in his calling and training of his disciples?

3. Ask God to give you spiritual eyes to see beyond the outward appearance and sense the heart of potential team members. Visible strengths and worldly standards are much easier to notice in other people. Yet we know that the heart of a person is much more important. Do you have a series of questions you can ask to probe for the inner qualities you are looking for? Start now to write helpful questions. Try them out in conversations with people. Refine them to be more effective.

4. Have you settled your own commitment not to lead based on authority that comes merely from the position you hold? Are you willing to be a servant to all? Does your leadership flow from your submission to God's call and Kingdom?

5. Have you thought about how you will "wash the feet" of your team members? Will you literally wash their feet in a ceremony? Will you schedule and budget in your ministry to recognize and honor them? Will your prayer letters and ministry reports highlight what you are doing? Or, what your team is doing?

Chapter Nine: Ask Courageously

1. Do you believe that God is calling you to invest your life in yo ur ministry vision? Do you also believe that he is calling others to invest financially to make it happen? Fund-raising for ministry is the process of finding the people God is calling to invest. Are you prepared to consider as part of your ministry to find those God is calling and showing them how their investment will promote the Kingdom of God?

2. Do you view your financial supporters as part of the ministry team, just as your fellow-workers in the ministry are part of the team? If it truly is a God-centered vision, it will

manifest itself as a cooperative effort of many of God's diverse people.

3. Are you personally embarrassed to ask people for help? If so, is this a matter of personal pride or a matter of philosophy of ministry? Are you prepared to accept sacrificial donations from very poor people as part of God's provision? Work through the nine Biblical principles of this chapter to reconsider any reluctance to allow others to participate in your vision.

4. People give differently and for different reasons:

Some give consistently, setting aside money from each paycheck to invest in the Kingdom of God.

Some give to vision, carefully selecting ministries they believe in and wanting maximum "bank for the buck."

Some give to crisis, waiting until there is an obvious need that their resources can meet.

Some give impulsively, responding to an emotional appeal or a particular prompting from God.

Do you have a strategy for identifying an individual's specific approach to giving and providing them with the right kind of request? Are you able to design a general request for support in a way that will attract all kinds of givers to respond?

5. Is your ultimate reliance for meeting the needs of your ministry in God himself and his ability to supply? Or, are you counting on your fund-raising experience or skill? Do you believe that God will lead you to those through whom he plans to provide?

Chapter Ten: Kingdom Perspective

1. What is your plan to "seek first the Kingdom of God and his righteousness"? Very few of us are wired to do this already.

We need to take deliberate steps in that direction. How do you remind yourself to give priority to God and his Kingdom? How do you protect against the tendency to seek recognition and credit for yourself? Have you specifically given permission to any family member or friend to question you about activities that seem to be self-promoting?

2. Review the benefits of putting the Kingdom first, listed in this chapter. Do you agree with them simply because you know that is the correct Christian answer? Or, are you truly sold on the values of Kingdom perspective?

3. When you share your vision or engage in ministry, do people respond with comments such as "Wow, he is so devoted!" or "What great insight she has!" or "I wish I could be more like that!"? Or, do they respond with "What a great God we serve!" or "What a gracious gospel God has given us!"? Discuss various ways we can direct our ministry to cause people to think more highly of God. How can we contribute to the goal of seeing the knowledge of the glory of the Lord filling the whole earth?

4. Do you experience joy in your ministry? Or, do you find it a continual struggle? Burn-out, frustration, and worry will follow you if you focus on maintaining your own image or trying to meet the world's standards of success. Explain how striving can be turned to thriving when we change our focus to building God's Kingdom. How would our attitudes be different? What methods would change? Would our urgency be any less? Would we feel less pressure to perform in the power of the flesh?

5. How does a Kingdom perspective make our ministry more about being fruitful in the ways that God has made us and called us? How does it relieve us of the compulsion to make things turn out the way we want them to? How does it empower our

leadership of others, allowing our team members to be fruitful in their own unique ways?

Chapter Eleven: Absolute Confidence in God

1. What character from the Bible do you look to as a hero? What was it about that person that exhibited faith in God? What would it look like in your life and ministry if you could consistently demonstrate that confidence? How has God equipped you through gifts, abilities, experiences, and understanding of God's character to lead in a similar way?

2. Do you have other role models from church history, the history of missions, or your own acquaintances that encourage you to trust fully in God and to venture into Kingdom work by God's power? Remember that we don't select role models on the basis of their perfection. All of us as humans have sinful tendencies and the potential of failing God. But we can all serve as an example to others to rely on the power of the Holy Spirit through fruitfulness and failure alike.

3. Has God allowed you to experience failure? Jesus did this for his disciples as an act of Kingdom leadership. Our tendency to rely on our own wisdom and strength often results in noticeable failures. Perhaps our failures are the preparation for our greatest means of glorifying God, if they teach us to stop depending on ourselves and rest completely on God.

4. How does our cultural background hinder us from trusting absolutely in God? Were you raised in a culture that has a natural explanation for everything that happens? Do you approach every day with an expectation that God is going to be active? Or, do you assume that if anything good is going to occur you will have to do it yourself? Immerse yourself in the culture of Scripture as a correcting influence for the weaknesses of your background. Pray for a divine perspective on the promises and provision of God in your life.

5. In some parts of the world today, people who trust completely in God face severe persecution. Believers under persecution may seem to have a greater confidence in God and his promises (by necessity). Other believers live in places where no one cares or notices--or where their service is honored. Do these believers have a harder time trusting God? Is your own trust level the result of your circumstances or the result of your experience of God's faithfulness?

Chapter Twelve: Spouse Shares the Vision

1. If you are married and have a family, have you come to agreement about the place your ministry vision will have in your family? Obviously, a person with a family has responsibilities for family members, not only for ministry. But a family that has worked through the vision and its requirements as it would affect the rest of the family has a huge head start. It is important, not only that they agree with you because that is expected, but that good, honest communication has been shared about the impact of ministry on the family and of the family on the ministry.

2. If you are not yet married, have you considered how the choice of a spouse could radically benefit or impair your ability to pursue the vision for Kingdom ministry God has called you to?

3. Is it possible for a husband and wife to have unity about the vision when they are involved in separate ministries, rather than both involved in the same ministry? God's Kingdom is not hindered by different family members using their different gifts and callings in different ministries. But it can be hindered if there are unspoken assumptions about priorities within the family. Special difficulty arises when a family member feels like God is their rival for the affection and time of the loved one.

4. In an earlier chapter, we saw how marriage is compared to a "yoke" that harnesses two animals together in partnership. How have you seen agreement or disagreement in your family about the goals and side-effects of your teamwork?

5. Just to make sure, revisit the discussion with your spouse about the role of the Kingdom of God in your family dynamics. Perhaps this should be done on an annual basis. One spouse is not free to assume the authority to choose how the family will function without the process of give and take. If you have children, especially as they get older, the Kingdom vision will affect their lives as well. Make sure you take time to share the vision, listen to concerns, and adjust the family schedule along the way.

About the Author

Dr. Saji Lukos is the Founder of Reaching Indians Ministries International (RIMI—USA), and Mission India (MI—India). His educational background includes a Master's degree in business, a Master of Divinity (Missions) from Trinity International University in Deerfield IL, and a Doctorate in Ministry from Bethel University in St. Paul MN.

Today RIMI/MI has become a major mission in India reaching people in every state of India with the message of Christ through three programs-Evangelism and Church Planting, Leadership and Compassion. Over 1500 missionaries are serving with Mission India. In addition to it, there a major seminary Nagpur (www.mits-india.org) and 29 Bible schools. Saji's passion is to raise up 100,000 Christ-like leaders within the next twenty years. Thus he is intentionally raising up 1000 pastors/leaders who will develop 100 leaders within the next 10-20 years.

Saji and Mony live in Round Lake Beach, IL, USA. They have a grown-up daughter Maryann, who is a school teacher in Waukegan.

Also by Saji Lukos

Transformed for a Purpose

Transformed for a Purpose is a compelling dramatic narrative of how God rescued a man and his family from the bondage of Satan to impact a nation with the Gospel of Jesus Christ.

Dr. Lukos writes with passion from an experience with Christ that overflows through the book. His story will both inspire and challenge the reader to greater resolve to seek first the Kingdom.

The One True God

The One True God is a masterful compilation of compelling stories how the One True God intervened in the lives of desperate men and women.

In this book, Saji with help of his associate writer Susan Lester, shares how lives that were once filled with revenge and murder are profoundly changed into a life filled with love and mercy. From death to life; from sickness to health; each story is unique and proof of the miraculous love of the One True God.

For more information about RIMI and to find out about other materials available, please visit

www.RIMI.org

You can also contact us at:

RIMI
1949 Old Elm Road
Lindenhurst, IL 60046, USA
847.265.0630
info@rimi.org

Please cut along dotted line

Kingdom Leadership
Order Form

I would like to help the ministry by sponsoring:

❒ **Child** ❒ **Missionary:** ❒ $30 ❒ $60 ❒ $120

❒ **Bicycle** $100 ❒ **Motorbike** $1,500

❒ **Where Most Needed** $___________

Please send me ____ more books at $17.95 + $4.50 Ship/Hndl each

for a total of $__________ (Call for quantity shipping rates)

Total Funds Enclosed $___________

Name

Address

Address

City / State / Zip Code

Phone

Praises and Prayers

Email

Credit Card: ❒ Visa ❒ MasterCard ❒ American Express ❒ Discover

Name as it appears on Card

Number Expiration Date Total

Signature

RIMI
1949 Old Elm Road, Lindenhurst, IL 60046
Phone: 847.265.0630 Fax: 847.265.0642
Email: ministry@RIMI.org Web: www.RIMI.org

Please make checks payable to RIMI
RIMI is a 501(c)(3) organization and all donations, except for books are tax deductable. A receipt will be sent for those items that qualify.

Please cut along dotted line

Kingdom Leadership
Order Form

I would like to help the ministry by sponsoring:

❒ **Child** ❒ **Missionary:** ❒ $30 ❒ $60 ❒ $120

❒ **Bicycle** $100 ❒ **Motorbike** $1,500

❒ **Where Most Needed** $____________

Please send me ____ more books at $17.95 + $4.50 Ship/Hndl each

for a total of $__________ (Call for quantity shipping rates)

Total Funds Enclosed $____________

Name

Address

Address

City / State / Zip Code

Phone

Praises and Prayers

Email

Credit Card: ❒ Visa ❒ MasterCard ❒ American Express ❒ Discover

Name as it appears on Card

Number Expiration Date Total

Signature

RIMI
1949 Old Elm Road, Lindenhurst, IL 60046
Phone: 847.265.0630 Fax: 847.265.0642
Email: ministry@RIMI.org Web: www.RIMI.org

Please make checks payable to RIMI
RIMI is a 501(c)(3) organization and all donations, except for books are tax deductable. A receipt will be sent for those items that qualify.